Yale's Ironmen

PRINCETON ATHLETIC NEWS
YALE
GAME
NOVEMBER 17, 1934
PRICE 25 CENTS

Yale's Ironmen

A Story of Football & Lives In The Decade of The Depression & Beyond

William N. Wallace

iUniverse, Inc.
New York Lincoln Shanghai

Yale's Ironmen
A Story of Football & Lives In The Decade of The Depression & Beyond

iUniverse books may be ordered through booksellers or by contacting:

iUniverse
2021 Pine Lake Road, Suite 100
Lincoln, NE 68512
www.iuniverse.com
1-800-Authors (1-800-288-4677)

Photo credits: DeAngelis collection; Wallace collection, Yale archives.
Cover design by Tom Burns, grandson of the author.

ISBN-13: 978-0-595-35925-7 (pbk)
ISBN-13: 978-0-595-67296-7 (cloth)
ISBN-13: 978-0-595-80379-8 (ebk)
ISBN-10: 0-595-35925-6 (pbk)
ISBN-10: 0-595-67296-5 (cloth)
ISBN-10: 0-595-80379-2 (ebk)

Printed in the United States of America

For Jim DeAngelis and Jerry Roscoe
who made it possible.

Content

Acknowledgments

Luck deserves the first credit…lucky enough to have known Jim DeAngelis for so many years and finally to have listened to his urging to record the Ironmen. Similarly to have renewed a comradeship with Jerry Roscoe who had put to paper his remarkable recall…and never threw anything away.

Geoff Zonder never tosses either. He collects, as The Archivist for Yale Athletics on Tower Parkway in New Haven. Larry Kelley is alive there.

Bob Barton, a newspaperman and Old Grad (Yale '57), has lived the peaks and valleys of the New Haven *Register*…an editor and writer in sports…and Yale football with equal grace and skill. He edited my copy and we are ready for any challenges.

'Old Yale' Friends: Ted Blair, Marty Dwyer, Jack Field, Bob Hall, Chet LaRoche, Walter Levering, Charlie Loftus, Fred Loeser, Win Lovejoy Sr. and Jr., Gould Martin, Century Milstead, Mal Stevens, Bill Stack, George Trevor, Kim Whitehead, et al.

Introduction

When to Cheer...When to Shut Up

A handsome girl who had come down from Smith College described a fall football Saturday at Princeton as an occasion so splendid as to be regal, royal. "I felt like a princess," said Gloria Conn in retrospection.

"Then I looked around and saw a lot of other princesses."

Miss Conn's tenure as a Princeton princess came in the 1940's after World War II, a golden time on many a campus. The university had had no women undergraduates since its founding in 1746 as the College of New Jersey, nor would it have any until 1969. Women, as social companions, were invited...imported.

Thus favored, they made considerable effort to reach the Princeton scene...or somewhat similar ones at Yale, at Harvard, Dartmouth and other all-boy colleges. There was the lesser nearby Amherst, a déuxieme invitation for Smith girls.

Miss Conn, and a handful of other Smith sensations, arose at 5 A.M. in Northampton, Mass., to catch the New Haven Railroad's southbound express at Springfield that would deposit them at Princeton Junction six hours later. Then came "the last mile," the quaint two-car train that ran from The

Junction into Princeton proper, a bouncy 12-minute rail experience that exists to this day.

"You were nervous," said Miss Conn. "Did you look okay? Had that pimple gone away? Would your date be there to meet you? Or had he gotten so besotted the night before as to forget?"

Upon returning Sunday night the custom in Miss Conn's residential house there, the small one called Henshaw, was that the girls who had been on the road assemble and each give an unvarnished account of her weekend: all its thrills or gaffes…the bold beau or the bumbling boy.

"Princeton was always so beautiful," she said. "The courtyards, the arches, the walkways, the trees in color. And the parties…it was hard not to have a good time. No matter how dim the date."

Well, what about the football?

"You learned quickly when to cheer," she said. "And when to shut up."

1

In The Beginning...

In the beginning there was Princeton and Rutgers. Those two played American football's first intercollegiate match in 1869 and four years later Princeton and Yale commenced their rivalry. By 1876 the Princeton-Yale games had become annual affairs, initially in Hoboken, N.J., but mostly in New York, uptown at 155th Street's old Polo Grounds and then at nearby Manhattan Field beginning in 1891.

These early contests were most often staged on Thanksgiving Day and, in the annals of American spectator sports, they became New York's first such spectacles. The crowds grew larger, 30,000 or so, and more colorful too according to the newspapers' front-page accounts plus the sketches in the weeklies, Leslie's and Harper's.

The Yale headquarters was at the Fifth Avenue Hotel in mid-town and Princeton's nearby at The Murray Hill.* Around ten in the morning the horse-drawn coaches, each embellished with

---

* "The camp followers and neutrals convened in the lobby of the Hoffman House. They made bets and they made noise. They were kept within reasonable bounds by Billy Edwards, former prize fighter who was a sort of guardian of the hotel. Billy mixed tact, personality and muscle in proportions sufficient unto the protection of furniture and glassware."...Tim Cohane in *The Yale Football Story*.

blue or orange and black colors, began a gala parade north up Fifth Avenue to Harlem River Drive and to the field of play.

Afterward the city's restaurants, hotels and theaters were filled with mirth and clamor from the football crowds. Those newspaper and magazine illustrations of the era depict stylish young men and women having some very good times.

However, the post-game throngs one year after another became so boisterous, so obstreperous that the New York merchants complained. And the police were tossing youths...Princeton, Yale or whatever...into station-house coolers.

So the games after 1896 went more comfortably home to campus sites at New Haven and Princeton where they remain. Except when the series was interrupted by war, 1917–1918 and 1944, the parties never ceased.

In the collective Princeton football psyche the game against Yale has been forever foremost, the one involving similar yet competitive institutions 130 miles apart. The Yale game comes in mid-November but alas as the penultimate of the season. The finale is against Dartmouth which means a sag and, according to Ivy League scheduling dictates, a long trip to Hanover, New Hampshire, every other year which few Princetonians undertake.

Smug Yale has had eternally two suitors for a gala November season's ending and, apart from a few exceptions, Harvard has won out. *The Game* became the pretentious title in the 1940's for that concluding match.* Such hyperbole has

---

* I credit Charles Loftus, Yale's imaginative sports information director and no alumnus, with the invention of the label in 1947. He passed it on to renowned sports columnist Red Smith of the New York *Herald Tribune* and others of that ilk. Smith liked the preposterous presumption and milked it. How do I know? While an undergraduate then, I was Loftus' lone assistant.

helped put about 50,000 spectators in the Yale Bowl every other autumn providing the Ivy League with its largest football assembly by far.

But Princeton was first. There have been 127 Princeton-Yale matches over 131 years through 2004, and never mind which has won the most.* About halfway through this epoch came the 1934 match, the most memorable of all in several ways.

Gloria Conn, my date at the 1949 game and to whom I proposed matrimony unsuccessfully as midnight neared, missed the 1934 contest. But I did not and, like a marriage, it marked my life. Sometimes we become what we are on account of a kiss, a song, a shove…or a contest, a game.

This long-ago football game that moved me so was won by Yale when it wasn't supposed to be. Since then I've seen hundreds of contests of all kinds and participated in a few. This one still sticks because of its heroic layer…the victors numbering 11 athletes, only 11.

With the odds 5 to 1…in some cases as high as 10 to 1…in favor of undefeated and mighty Princeton, the Yale team began and finished with the same players, each enduring for the entire 60 minutes. Forever after they were known as The Ironmen.

That was an uncommon feat then, one never repeated in major college football circles thereafter and beyond contemplation in contemporary times. Now players enter and exit football games after every play in such dizzying array it's hard for spectators to know who's on stage and who's off.

---

* Suffice to say there have been more games played in this rivalry than in any other with the exception of Lafayette-Lehigh, the near-neighbors who did not commence until 1884 and often clashed twice in the same season.

College teams will have from 60 to 100 young men in uniform on game day.

Yale went down to Princeton…by train…that November of 1934 with just 28 players composing an ordinary team that had lost half of its six games. Fifty three thousand spectators overflowed Palmer Stadium and one was a ten-year-old lad taken to the game by his father. The only score came in the first quarter when Larry Kelley reached high in the sky to bring down a pass and then eluded three Tiger tacklers to complete a 48-yard touchdown play.

Etched forever in my memory…for I was the ten-year-old…is the extended Kelley in white helmet and blue jersey grabbing at the football.

Much was made of the event, the New York newspapers full with accounts the next day. From those I made a connection that set my life on a trail. I was a small boy…49 pounds for oh, so many years…who would never play football for Yale. But maybe I could write up the games, like Robert Fulton Kelley there in the New York *Times*.

Larry Kelley, a sophomore that season, was a famous man two years later, an All-America selection and awarded the Heisman Trophy as college football's foremost player. A series of bons mots was attributed to him…wisecracks in the heat of competition…by imaginative sports writers like George Trevor of *The Sun* in New York. A Yale man, Trevor thought it was his right to put words in the mouths of the Bulldogs. And Kelley could be glib.

As a result of the process he didn't think much of journalists. Kelley did understand that those tales were integral to his popularity, to being voted the Heisman award. In October 1937 the *Saturday Evening Post*, a magazine with a huge coast-to-coast readership, published two autobiographical articles by Kelley…“with George Trevor”…and they made him famous forevermore.

I could never let go of The Ironmen. For me that 1934 setting was like looking at a stunning portrait by John Singer Sargent and craving to know more of the silent subjects.

My satisfaction came in time.

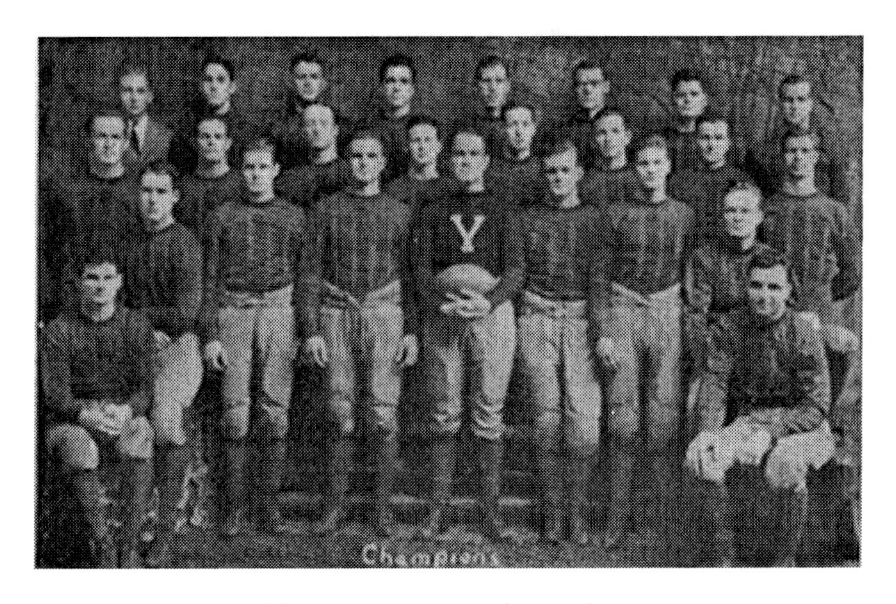

The 1934 Yale team's formal portrait.

In the 1970's a freelance writer named Norman Macht wrote up a good nostalgia story about The Ironmen and tried without success to sell it to *Sports Illustrated* among other magazines.

The manuscript came into the hands of Kim Whitehead, The Ironmen's fullback, who passed it along to me to see what I could do. Whitehead was an acquaintance and a neighbor, in Fairfield, Conn. Being knowledgeable about magazine rejections, I wasn't keen to shop elsewhere. So I put the piece away, but not before reading it carefully.

Macht, with his digging, had unmasked The Ironmen's game. He had bountiful detail, mentioning Yale's secret scouting report on Princeton…76 pages thick.*

More years went by. Then a freelance named Dan Armstrong wrote a look-backward piece about The Ironmen for a tabloid called *College & Pro Football Newsweekly*. In it was the claim that the winning touchdown pass caught by Kelley had been a mistake…improvised because of a bad pass from the center, Jimmy DeAngelis, that had wrecked the original play.

Someone sent DeAngelis the article and he was enraged. "I never made a bad pass from center in my life," he shouted to whoever was nearby. DeAngelis knew me as a reporter who covered a lot of Yale games and for a while he thought I had written the article. He insisted that I correct the egregious mistake, assuming all a writer had to do was wave a wand.

But I did feel an inner push and began to poke around.

Who were The Ironmen? What had been their path to that football stadium on that November afternoon?

First, the context. In the Depression era of the 1930's only about 10 to 12 per cent of high school graduates were inclined to attempt college. For those who aimed at the academically testing eastern private universities, many still requiring skills in Greek and Latin, a common route was high school and then a prep year or two. That's why the name, preparatory school. And this was the route common to the Ironmen.

What of Yale then?

It was made up of 3,000 male undergraduates and tuition cost just $450. A bunch of rich kids? Hardly. Several Ironmen had scholarships and Kelley, for one, was a waiter at the football training table.

How did that game play out? What happened afterward?

---

* No copy exists that I could find, not even in Yale's athletic archives.

The Ironmen posed on their practice field 4 days after defeating Princeton. L to R. (front) Kelley, Wright, Grosscup, DeAngelis, Curtin, Scott, Train, (rear) Morton, Whitehead, Roscoe, Fuller.

2

Princeton Was Goliath, Yale David

Allison Danzig was a small man with a sweet heart. A sports-writer for the New York *Times* for almost half a century, he embodied kindliness…soft, enhancing words for his subjects. They were for the most part football players, oarsmen, and racquet players of all descriptions.*

The next-to-last game he wrote up for the *Times* before retirement was in 1967 when Yale defeated Harvard, 24-20, in part because the Harvard fullback lost a fumble at the Yale 10-yard line with 56 seconds left and the Crimson driving for a winning touchdown.

Danzig didn't mention the fumble until the 17th paragraph of his 1,200-word story and never revealed the Harvard man's name. Didn't want to embarrass him. He wrote simply, "The ball popped out of the carrier's hands."

It was my task to produce a supplementary story taking in the locker room scene, and I led off with this key play. I

---

* An aside: Danzig was the only accredited journalist able to describe with accuracy the playing and outcome of the game of Court Tennis, a sport that had in his time only three facilities—those courts with their galleries, penthouses and dedans. The most prominent one belonged to the elegant Racquet & Tennis Club with its imposing posture on New York's Park Avenue at 52nd Street, where he was coddled.

named the fumbler, wrote about what might have been, and quoted his sympathetic teammates. Two brands of journalism, classic and modern, and on that day at least I was unsure of the need for the second.

Danzig's gentleness extended to his courtly presence, that of an unobtrusive man who knew his football having been a tiny varsity player, a scrub, for Cornell.

He was never chosen to join the board of the Cornell *Sun*, the university's daily newspaper, although having exhibited ability during a tryout. The distinguished E.B. White, a classmate and *Sun* staffer, deplored this oversight in later years and suspected that Danzig's being Jewish had something to do with the rejection.

Danzig's passion for college football became conspicuous upon Prentice-Hall's 1957 publication of his classic, *The History of American Football.*[*] Here is what he had to say about the Princeton teams of 1933 through 1935:

"One of the most brilliant football classes ever to matriculate at Princeton entered Nassau's halls of learning in 1932. For four years it furnished the sinews of Tiger teams, and just once did the members experience defeat. As freshmen and as sophomores and seniors on the varsity eleven they defeated every opponent. Under the expert coaching of Herbert Orrin (Fritz) Crisler the Princeton varsity put together three of the greatest years Nassau has enjoyed on the gridiron.

---

[*] My autograph copy says, "To Bill. You carry the ball now." Although flattered I failed Allison, becoming immersed in professional football, which he disdained. I heard him once tell an editor, "Our readers are not interested in THAT." At the time the Giants had New York enthralled, including *The Times*' circulation director, chief accountant and photo editor.

"Their one setback came in 1934 in the most shocking reversal of the season...their loss to Yale and Larry Kelley."

Danzig, in compiling his book, wrote letters to dozens of eminent coaches and included their responses. There was one from Crisler, dated May 12, 1952, in which he mentioned his 1933 and 1935 teams, citing the backfield..."Kadlic, Constable, LeVan and Spofford had a great scoring punch"...but skipping 1934.*

A contemporary account of the Princeton team came from the Boston *Herald's* Arthur Sampson, a respected authority: "Offensively the Princeton line operates like a steam roller. It charges forward as one man or chops the defensive line to pieces with cross-blocks. Defensively it is so ruthlessly powerful that it makes the Tigers a scoring threat even when the opponents have the ball."

So that is what Princeton was all about...perfect for three consecutive seasons except for that damned blotch, that Yale thing in 1934.

Crisler, in the Danzig book, cited 1933's 20-0 victory over "the Columbia team that went to the Rose Bowl," as "one of the finest clutch performances during my years at Princeton."

That Columbia team's 7-0 upset of Stanford, in the rain at Pasadena on January 1, 1934, had resonated at Princeton.

After the varsity defeated Lehigh, 54-0, for the Tigers' 15th consecutive victory on November 10, 1934, a petition was circulated around the campus the following Monday, a petition that attracted 837 signatures, or more than a third of the undergraduate student body.

---

* Crisler also said that on occasion, late at night, he would receive phone calls from writer F. Scott Fitzgerald, a fervent Princeton alumnus, offering trick plays to use against Yale.

The petition, an inspiration of four sophomores, suggested that when the regular season was over the Princeton team play a post-season game against Minnesota...No. 1 in the newfangled Associated Press poll "of experts around the country"...or Pittsburgh, No. 4 in the ranking.*

Princeton was No. 5, and the authors assumed that rank would remain the same, or go even higher, after the two remaining games were finished, against Yale and Dartmouth at home in Palmer Stadium.

The proposal had two prongs. The first was that with a national power would be played for charity, the undergraduates being well aware that the nation was deep into The Great Depression. The mayor of Detroit, Frank Murphy, had recently told a Senate subcommittee that the city's relief rolls included doctors, lawyers, ministers, and "two families after whom streets are named."

Hours after Princeton beat Lehigh, a 45-year-old real estate broker had shot himself in an Atlantic City hotel room, 70 miles from Princeton. He had left a note that said, "I couldn't stand the Depression."

The unemployment rate was 21.7 per cent, meaning 12 million without jobs. Two million men had joined the Public Works Administration, the make-work construction outfit subsidized by the Federal government, according to Secretary of the Interior Harold Ickes.

So unemployment was up while prices were down. In New York City, a Princetonian on the town could buy dinner at Rosoff's off Times Square for 75 cents, a ticket to the rodeo

---

* Stanford and Alabama, which would meet in the Rose Bowl with Alabama winning, were No. 2 and No. 3.

at Madison Square Garden for $1, and the best seat Saturday night at the Metropolitan Opera for $4.

The charity angle had precedents going back three years. To raise quick money for the unemployed, exhibition games were played after the regular 1931 season ended. There had been seventeen of these involving colleges in every part of the country, and the ones in which Princeton and Yale participated were different in being abbreviated…two periods of 12 minutes each.

In the Yale Bowl on December 5, before a cold crowd of 23,000, Brown was the winner over Dartmouth and Yale defeated Holy Cross. The Bulldogs were the victors against Brown in the finale of the tournament, which raised $46,000 for what was called "unemployment relief."

A similar affair took place the following Wednesday in New York's Yankee Stadium, where Columbia beat Princeton in 24 minutes and Cornell bested Pennsylvania. The deciding match, Columbia against Cornell, was called off because the weather was so miserable, rainy and cold. Only about 8,000 were in the stands and no official figures were given for attendance or receipts.

The second prong of the proposal was what the undergraduates really had in mind. They stated such a game against a powerhouse like Minnesota or Pittsburgh would "show that Princeton has a real football team," and "quell propaganda that Princeton is afraid to play a team recognized as one of the best in the country."

In a letter to the editor of the *Daily Princetonian*, the four sophomores wrote, "This year's Princeton football team has a schedule which can only be described as of the cream-puff variety." Besides Lehigh the cream puffs had been Amherst, Cornell, Harvard, Washington and Lee, and Williams.

The Rose Bowl matter remained fresh too. Following 1933's undefeated season Princeton had been asked informally whether it would accept an invitation to play in the famous game at Pasadena on New Year's Day, if proffered. Through channels Princeton said no, or so the undergraduates and alumni came to believe.

The invitation went to Columbia and, after the Lions won to wide acclaim, the team was given a ticker tape parade down Broadway in New York. *What if*, grumbled some miffed sons of Old Nassau.

Although Princeton in 1934 was once more being touted in the sports pages as a worthy Rose Bowl candidate, the editors of the *Daily Princetonian* came down hard against the petition for the charity game as did Professor Burnham N. Dell. He was the chairman of the university council on athletics and the person to whom the petition had been addressed.

The editorial said the proposal "for the purpose of giving a crowd having little connection to either university a few thrills is repugnant."

Professor Dell said he welcomed the petition because, "Campus opinion has been helpful time and again in the formation of athletic policies." Then he cited a guideline in a dual agreement with Yale: "No postseason contests for the purpose of settling sectional or other championships shall be permitted."

The professor added, "When (college athletics) tend to usurp more than their rightful share of interest and attention, they become harmful and should be restricted."

The issue of rightful share had already been debated through the first third of the 20th century and would continue into the next.

3

They Trying To Scare Us?

All around Professor Dell, interest in Saturday's Yale game was building, rightful or otherwise. Every ticket, priced at $3.50, had been sold and Palmer Stadium would be full for the first time since 1928. The athletic department was pondering the possibility of adding wooden stands at the open end to raise the seating capacity from 52,000 to 61,000.*

And the Pennsylvania Railroad was calculating how many special trains to schedule for the Saturday morning runs from New York and Philadelphia into the seldom-used yards near the stadium.

It was hard to know what all the excitement was about. Princeton, which had last lost a game in 1932, was a big favorite, having outscored six opponents, 242 points to 18. Coach Crisler had a sports dynasty going, and it was said you could hardly walk two blocks down Nassau Street without bumping into at least two former prep school football captains.**

---

* One small stand was erected, seating about 1,000. There wasn't time enough for the others.

** Michigan played Southern California in the 1977 Rose Bowl game and I was standing in a line underneath that great stadium—a Yale Bowl copy—waiting for the elevator to go up to the press box. Murray Olderman, an all-knowing colleague, told me the man right

Crisler's opposite at Yale was Raymond (Ducky) Pond, a 31-year-old first-year coach so doubted by his athletic director, Malcolm Farmer, that he had been given an assistant coach with almost as much authority...and salary ($8,000). That was 41-year-old Earle (Greasy) Neale, whose considerable background included an eight-season major-league baseball career.

Neale had led the winning Cincinnati Reds in hitting (.357) in the 1919 World Series against the infamous Chicago Black Sox. He had also been the head football coach at Muskingum, West Virginia Wesleyan (his alma mater), Marietta, Washington & Jefferson, Virginia and West Virginia in that order, 1915–1933. At Washington & Jefferson in Washington, Pa., which then had a student body of 500 undergraduates, his 1921 team went unbeaten and played California to a scoreless tie in the 1922 Rose Bowl game.

The Presidents were such an unknown quantity on the West Coast that a California sportswriter wrote before the contest, "All I know is both of them are dead."

After Yale, Neale coached the Philadelphia Eagles* for a decade, and twice the Eagles won National Football League

---

in front was Crisler, the retired Michigan athletic director and revered old coach whom I had never met. I introduced myself and said, "Say, is it true you had 30 prep school football captains on those teams at Princeton?" He looked at me as though I had insulted his mother, scoffed, turned his back, and that was that.

* Alexis (Lex) Thompson, a wealthy Chicagoan and an undergraduate in the class of 1936 during Neale's first two seasons at Yale, bought control of the Eagles' franchise and made Neale head coach. As a varsity cheerleader on the sidelines he had seen and heard Neale in action. He was also varsity hockey manager and stated his residence as the Ambassador West Hotel in Chicago.

championships, 1948 and 1949. He is in several football halls of fame. Greasy?

Growing up in Parkersburg, W. Va., Neale had called a neighbor's child "dirty." The retort was "greasy" and it stuck.

Ducky Pond was a townie from Torrington, Conn., who polished his academics at Hotchkiss before entering Yale in 1921. A spectacular run for a touchdown in the rain and mud of Harvard Stadium in 1923 inspired the nickname. He was an organized, quiet and popular coach who had been a Yale assistant to his two predecessors, Reg Root and Mal Stevens.

Raymond (Ducky) Pond

Besides Neale, Pond had two more proficient assistants in Denny Myers, the line coach, and Ivan Williamson, end coach. Myers later was the head coach at Boston College and Williamson at Wisconsin.

Jim DeAngelis, the Ironmen's center and afterward a college coach for 15 years, said in reflection, "No one had a staff like ours."

Yale was unimpressive in a 14-7 defeat at home to Georgia on November 10. Other losses were to Army and Columbia, while the team had beaten Brown decisively, Dartmouth and Pennsylvania barely.

That schedule, which Trevor and other writers deemed as the most difficult the Bulldogs had ever undertaken, had been formulated by Farmer, a former Yale player of the class of 1904 and also a businessman who sought to increase the Yale Bowl revenues. They had fallen sharply following the departure after 1931 of the breathtaking Albie Booth, the tiny hometown halfback, and due to the ongoing impact of the Depression.

Malcolm Farmer

Pond and Neale had shuffled nine linemen and seven backs through the autumn, the only constants having been halfback Strat Morton and the two ends, Lawrence Morgan Kelley and Robert (Choo Choo) Train.

It came down to this. The Yale coaches had only 18 players they felt they could trust in a varsity game…eleven regulars and seven backups from a squad of 65 that had reported in September to training camp.*

Matchbox cover

The contrast between Yale and Princeton was overt when the teams came on the field at Palmer Stadium. The visiting team had come out first and was scattered about, limbering

---

* One of several Pond innovations was an off-campus training site, this one being the venerable and hardy Yale crew camp on the Thames River at Gales Ferry, Conn. It exists all but untouched to this day but was abandoned by the football program following the intrusive 1938 hurricane.

up. After several minutes, from the open end into the stadium came a line of Tigers streaming down the home team's sideline. It was a very long line.

Meredith Scott, the Yale sophomore tackle, said, "I was crouching and I looked up and here came this troop. They were silhouetted against the sky and looked huge. They must have had the varsity, junior varsity, freshmen and the 150-pounders, everyone they could round up and put a uniform on."

Coach Crisler had his legions line up, shoulder to shoulder in black jerseys striped with those damned orange rings down the sleeves. And underneath was the bulk shoulder pad that made each of 66 Tigers large and intimidating.

These Goliaths stretched from one 10-yard line to the other. Crisler walked up and down, stopping to talk to a particular player while pointing over at one or more of the foe. By contrast the Davids…the Yales…were pitiful, only 28 in uniform. "What are they trying to do, scare us?" said Jim DeAngelis.

Merri Scott said to no one in particular, "They'll be running waves of subs in on us all day." He had no notion that Yale would present to Princeton just its one wave, one band of eleven players who would go without substitution, who would play all sixty minutes.

Against poor Lehigh, Crisler had unleashed three teams, one after the other. The stars were many—Gary LeVan, Pepper Constable and Ken Sandbach among the backs, Jack Weller, Mose Kalbaugh and Hugh MacMillan in the line.

Larry Kelley

If Yale had a star player, he was still emerging. The most likely candidate was Kelley, the tall sophomore who had deceptive speed and who could catch a pass thrown high or low.

4

Lindbergh and Crisler

In January, 1932, the foremost celebrity in the United States, Charles Lindbergh, and his wife, Anne, moved into a new home on an estate in Hopewell, N.J., eight miles from Princeton. On March 1 their infant son, Charles 3rd, was taken from his crib in the second-floor nursery during the night.

"Kidnap" became a familiar word among Americans.

On that day Fritz Crisler, head coach at the University of Minnesota in Minneapolis, had an appointment in Princeton to complete details about becoming the head of football there. Al Wittmer had been dismissed following a 1-7 season that included a 51-14 thrashing by Yale.

Crisler was driving down from New York in a car that he had borrowed. Nearing Princeton, he was surprised to be stopped at a roadblock set by the New Jersey state police and then interrogated. The officers were in search of clues to the kidnapping, of which Crisler knew nothing.

Fritz Crisler

"There I was driving alone in a car that wasn't my own," he recalled. "The police were concerned. It took a phone call before they would release me."*

His interest piqued, Princeton's new coach followed the turns of events along with millions of others. On March 12, he was driving to a restaurant in Hopewell, and on the way Crisler passed a man driving a hay cart pulled by a mule.

He was to learn that this man shortly thereafter had pulled off the road and gone into the woods to relieve himself. There he found the dead body of Charles Lindbergh 3rd.

---

* The call was to Hack McGraw of Princeton's McGraw-Hill publishing family. He owned the car.

So Crisler was attentive when Bruno Richard Hauptmann, an immigrant carpenter, was indicted for murder and kidnapping four days after his first game as Princeton's head coach the following October. That was a 75-0 rout of Amherst.

There was a lot going on in the Garden State that fall.

The ocean liner Morro Castle, heading for New York from Havana, ran aground and burned off Asbury Park with loss of 133 lives in September. The 11,000-ton ship washed up on the beach in erect posture and one of the autumnal undergraduate endeavors was to go over and view the spectacle.

At Newark the first commercial airport of consequence for the New York region commenced tempting operations. It was from there that a quartet of Yale juniors executed a courageous yet casual feat that had the campus agog.

They flew out to Detroit on the night of October 7 to take in the seventh and last game of a distinguished World Series matching the hometown Tigers and the St. Louis Cardinals, a team stamped by pitcher Dizzy Dean.

It has been said that they bet on the Cardinals and won enough to pay for the trip, then flew back to New Haven via Newark, missing only one day of classes. The stunt was written up in the Yale *Alumni Weekly*, but without names.

One of the four was quarterback Jerome Verity (Jerry) Roscoe's roommate, Louis (Lou) Walker, who half a century afterward attained recognition as U.S. President George Herbert Walker Bush's most visible uncle. Another, the instigator and a noted gambler, was Robert Barbour (Bob) Cooke, who in time became the sports editor of the New York *Herald Tribune*.*

---

* Cooke in 1957 hired me away from the New York *World-Telegram & Sun* to become the *Herald Tribune's* yachting editor among other things, at a 20 per cent pay raise by my demand.

Playboys. L.-R. Kim Whitehead, unknown,
Lou Walker, Bob Cooke, unknown.

The following Saturday, November 17, my father and I drove past this Newark airport just off U.S. Route 1 en route to Princeton and the Yale game. The airport held the interest of Lew Wallace Jr., a fan of flight. He was a not a sports fan, however, and I have no idea why he chose to go this game, other than being an alumnus, Class of 1914 Sheff, with a casual interest in Yale football. I was delighted.

It was a four-hour drive from where we lived in Rye, Westchester County, into and through New York City, under the Hudson River via the Holland Tunnel and up to the new General Pulaski Skyway, which swept across Jersey City and Kearny. Then came the trek to Princeton, passing along those telephone poles southward, an occasional hillock breaking the mid-Jersey plain. Interminable.

Our car was a pale green 1932 Ford Model A four-door sedan, a comedown for Lew Wallace, whose previous automobiles had included a Duesenberg and a Stutz, both made in his home city of Indianapolis, Indiana. Earlier in the year he had given up his seat on the New York Stock Exchange, and he was either unemployed or retired, supporting a wife and four children from his considerable yet diminishing inheritance that had come from the earnings of the 1880 novel *Ben Hur* written by his grandfather, General Lew Wallace.

The youngest child, Billy, was a nascent sports fan with more focus on baseball than football, for reason. The Wallaces from Indiana at the turn of the 20th century had built a fishing camp or cottage on Burt Lake, a modest loch near the top of Michigan's lower peninsula, along with other Hoosier luminaries, one of whom was Kenesaw Mountain Landis.

Judge Landis and his family were our next-door neighbors and friends through three generations. Landis, a federal judge in Chicago, had become the Commissioner of Baseball following the Black Sox scandal of 1919, a position he shared with the Wallaces by invitation to be his guests in his box when he came to New York for World Series games over many years.

On a rainy day in May, 1934, Commissioner Landis was in New York at the Polo Grounds to hand out to the Giants the rings they had earned by defeating the Washington Senators in the World Series of 1933. My father, mother and I, the unfledged 10-year-old, were invited, and when the game was called off the Judge took us into the Giants' clubhouse, where he handed out the rings to the players with humor and grace.

I was shy. But the athletes were friendly, smiling. Carl Hubbell and Mel Ott became my heroes forever.

The link to Yale football had a beginning in 1931 when I was taken to a game at the Bowl in company with my Rye playmate, John Hanes; his mother and my mother, best of friends; and a chauffeur who drove the Hanes' Isotta Franschini sedan and did the tailgating picnic tasks from a Fortnum & Mason wicker basket many years before the tail-gate word evolved.

Bob Lassiter, John Senior's nephew from the Hanes cotton-rich family of North Carolina, was a sophomore halfback for Yale that day and, two seasons later, its captain. The final score was 52-0, the opponent a pigeon that Yale had scheduled prior to the final two games that mattered, against Princeton and Harvard. The victim was tiny St. John's of Annapolis, an academic institution across the street from the Naval Academy and renowned for its great-books curriculum, not then nor ever for its jocks.

I recall nothing of the game itself, one in which Joe Crowley scored five touchdowns, a Yale record to this day. Kindly Agnes Hanes told me I'd remember the final score because it was the same as the number of playing cards in a deck. She was correct on both counts.

Years later I met in New York an administrator working for Commissioner Asa Bushnell and the Eastern College Athletic Conference, which had its headquarters in the Hotel Biltmore next to Grand Central Terminal. Danny Hill had played for the St. John's team that warm November day. He said he assumed his college had taken the game invitation for the money, the guarantee Yale would pay; that they went north with 18 players and near the end only eleven were still able to perform.

The handsome Lassiter came down from New Haven on occasion to the Hanes' estate, Westerleigh, in Rye and he included Johnny and Billy in his visit to the children's playroom far from the grownups. To me he was a god, a Yale god.*

While enduring Route 1 to Princeton, my father and I had no idea how seriously the Yale side had been preparing for this game. The Tigers, with all their pomposity and success, were a ripe target. So thought Robert A. (Bob) Hall, a graduate in 1930 who had won the major Y letter in 1927 and 1929 as a back-up quarterback. Hall was certainly not the first student of this American game…then only in its 66th year…but one of the most zealous.**

He had spent previous Saturdays in the stands with binoculars and notebook at Palmer Stadium where Princeton had played all but one of its six games. Former players joined him for one game or another, a total of nine contributing to what Hall handed over to Pond and Neale, the 76-page scouting report on the Tigers.

Hall's perception of how the Princeton halfbacks had responded to the punt formations of the opponents' offenses led Neale…"a perfectionist with an encyclopedic mind" as someone said…to set up the pass play for Jerry Roscoe and Kelley that would win the game for Yale.

---

* Left unsaid and unknown to me until years later was that Lassiter played the passive role in the death of an Army end, Richard Brinsley Sheridan, in Yale Bowl two weeks before the St. John's game. Lassiter was returning a kickoff when tackled by Sheridan head on. The Cadet's back was broken…two fractured vertebrae…and he died two days later.

** Hall served as Yale's director of athletics, 1950–1953.

5

A Little Surprise for Crisler

The daily practice reports in the newspapers during the week were predictable: "Princeton Tunes Elaborate Aerial Attack," "Yale Polishes Defense." The starting lineups, as given out by the head coaches, were there and Yale's was wrong on purpose.

Bernie Rankin, the fastest running back, was logically listed as the left halfback in the single-wing offense. But Stan Fuller would start there instead of Rankin because Fuller was a superb punter. The Pond-Neale strategy depended upon keeping the savage Princeton attack bottled up through punting…hopefully deep out-of-bounds kicks. That was hardly a big secret, but why not make a little surprise for Crisler?

The choice between Fuller and Rankin was a hard one for the coaches and dictated also by the substitution rules then in effect. Football's rules had been amended on an almost annual basis since the invention of the game by Princeton and Rutgers undergraduates in 1869. By 1934 the substitution rule was that a player once removed from a game could not return in the same quarter.

Of course the players played both offensively and defensively and had since the game was begun. "That's what made it so much fun, win or lose," recalled Jerry Roscoe. Unlimited substitution, allowing for specialists such as a player who did nothing but punt, would not come along until World War II.*

Yale had only 28 players...compared with Princeton's 46...and did not anticipate using many substitutes against the Tigers. Thus the coaches had to balance the worth of Rankin's speed against Fuller's punting. Yale had to have Fuller available throughout the game, to keep Princeton in a hole hopefully and Gary LeVan pinned down...if at all possible. LeVan, an Ohioan called the Steubenville Spook by Trevor, was swift and elusive.

Such limited substitution was a part of the mission of the college football rules committee to keep the destiny of the game out of the hands of the coaches and in the control of the players. Similarly, another rule forbade coaches to call plays or communicate in any way with the athletes on the field.

Coaching from the sidelines...the selection of offensive plays, for example...had been an issue since the turn of the century and the coaches continued to chip away at the prohibitions until, by 1967, they had disappeared. The consensus among coaches with regard to play-calling ran something like this: "Why should I trust my job to a 19-year-old kid?"

Greasy Neale was in charge of Yale's offense. Roscoe, in his account,** wrote, "Ducky Pond had been a great Yale

---

* Michigan, with Crisler as coach, introduced platoon football in a game against Army on October 13, 1945, substituting eight players for offense only and eight for defense. The procedure was widely copied and Army's Red Blaik called the units "platoons," the platoons of offensive and defensive specialists that make up the large squads of contemporary football.

** Richard Goldstein, author of "Ivy League Autumns," asked Roscoe and dozens of others for memories and recollections in 1995. Roscoe, on a yellow legal pad, wrote ingenuously 6, 556 words in 27 pages of which only a sliver were published. Roscoe made a copy.

player in the mid-1920's and an assistant coach ever since. I don't mean to denigrate him in the slightest, but it was Greasy Neale who had the football brains and experience that contributed in a major way to whatever success Yale enjoyed in the years he coached there.

"His West Virginia accent and his nickname tended to deflect on occasion what he was really all about."

That Neale could be crude in his coaching there was no doubt. After an unsatisfactory effort Neale might say, "You block like a sick whore getting off a pisspot." So Jim DeAngelis attested.

Yet Roscoe considered apt the commendations given Neale upon his induction into the College Football Hall of Fame in 1967: "His influence as a teacher of men and for the integrity of his character throughout his career…His contributions as a wizard strategist became legend."

Neale had given Yale a different offense, new to the Bulldogs, during the two weeks of spring practice in April, 1934. It was characterized as a spinner offense and Roscoe, the quarterback, did the spinning.

He said, "The primary conception of the offense, however, was for the quarterback to receive the ball, half spin in place so that his back was to the line of scrimmage, at which point there were a large number of things that could happen; handoff to the left halfback or fullback to run; fake handoff to the left halfback or fullback and give to the wing back coming around; as above but fake and keep to run right; fake to left halfback and or fullback, make a full spin and shovel pass to the wing back as he ran left close to line of scrimmage. And of course at any time the quarterback had the option of passing, or faking one or more handoffs and then passing."

The idea was to create uncertainty, hesitation, in the defense. Columbia had used such an offense in its Rose Bowl victory over Stanford. Wrote Roscoe: "Somehow Greasy was able to get ahold of two or three feet of film of Columbia's spin-handoff offense and he used to carry it around and study it at all sorts of odd times with a small magnifying glass. He swore he could improve on it.

"Greasy became very demanding in how I spun, how I used my hands and arms to either handoff or fake a hand-off and keep the ball. And he was equally meticulous in demanding the same care by both the fullback and wing back as either took the ball from the spinner, or on a fake looked like they had received the ball.

"In practice Greasy would make the four backs line up with no linemen except the center to snap the ball, and no defensive players at all. Four coaches would spread out yards apart and 10 or 15 yards down field, and have us call our own plays unknown to the coaches. We'd execute time after time until none of the coaches could tell who had the ball."

Roscoe's relationship with Neale began with that spring practice and continued during almost daily meetings until the term ended in June. Roscoe then went to Wyoming to work on a dude ranch and Neale followed him by mail from Lost Creek, W. Va.

"He wrote me several times during the summer with 10-15 questions which I had to answer back. Each question set up such things as down, position on field, score, wind, etc., etc. and I had to write him back and give him the play or optional play I would call, and why. He would then send the letter back telling if I was correct, or if I was wrong, and why.

"When practice started for the '34 season, the meetings were held daily except Sundays, including game day, and all of that continued through my last season in '35. Greasy would hold these meetings at any time of day or evening, to be sure none of us let them interfere with school classes, labs, etc.

"We became very close friends, which lasted until his death in 1973. I had played quarterback and safety for 3 years at Kent School and for 2 years at Yale before Greasy arrived, but the vast majority of what I learned about both strategy and execution came from him."

Thus Roscoe did not hesitate to call what became the winning touchdown play when the perfect situation came up late in the first period...third down on Princeton's 48-yard line and 12 yards to go for a first down. It was a punting situation. But Yale didn't punt.

6

The Yale Song

We refuse to be palavered
Into speaking well of Harvard,
Or of Williams, Dartmouth, MIT or Brown.
And our greatest scorn's evinced on
Any mentioning of Princeton,
While of Amherst we in chorus shout "thumbs down"!

We think there's nothing horrider
Than Holy Cross or Florida,
Cornell and Bowdoin are beyond the pale.
There's but one place, no place near it,
For the real collegiate spirit,
And that place...hats off all...is Eli Yale.

In these days when there's a scarcity
Of men who root for varsity,
It's good to know there are men alive who want to cheer and can.
For we Yale men watch each game
And like it just the same,
If it's Harvard, Notre Dame or simply Wesleyan.

When it comes to torch processions,
Rallies, songs and long pep sessions,
It is only at Old Eli...dear Old Eli...they prevail.
What a pity then that Yalesmen
Must all become bond salesmen,
And work for God, for Country, but most of all for kale.

Now all thanks to Mr. Harkness
For his expensive Gothic darkness.
Perhaps his rooms are gloomy but they're large.
And each of us acknowledges
The beauty of the colleges
That he's given to Old Eli...free of charge.

But if they think that in these cloisters,
We'll lead the lives of oysters,
Be studious and start to use our brain;
That in these halls so mediaeval
We will carefully shun all evil...
If they think that they'd better think again!

For we have to have our frolics
And our share of alcoholics;
And we're glad of any chance to break the academic quiet.
For our lives are pretty hideous
What with courses, lectures, mid-years;
And we really can't be blamed if from time to time we riot.

Oh, it always brings a snicker
When a Yale man speaks of liquor;

And the way we drink at football games is called a major sin.
That we shame our Alma Mater
Is merely idle chatter;
For that is why Yale Bowl was made...to hold Old Eli's gin.

Oh those lucky stiffs in Cambaridge
Don't spend their weekends playing bridge,
For Boston has the Copley and the Ritz.
And if they're overpowered
By the filth at the Old Howard,
They find in Boston aged Broadway hits.

But everyone goes ravin'
Mad, who stays long in New Haven.
You either go New York or go insane.
Ah but there the sly Manhattanites
And night-club owners fatten nights
On us who go back on the old milk train.

We would never never fail
To give a cheer for Yale,
The kind indulgent friend of our gilded flaming youth.
And we'd fire off scores of guns
To praise her noblest sons...
Rudy Vallee, Peter Arno and immortal Albie Booth.

We would die for dear Old Blue,
Though no one's asked us to.
And the Faculty is excellent, or so we have heard tell.

For five days out of seven Old Ell is a heaven.
But from Friday until Monday
*It's a good deal worse than Hell.**

This delicious lampoon of Yale that came down from Harvard contained truths. Edward S. Harkness, an 1897 Yale graduate whose father was an original Cleveland partner of John D. Rockefeller in the oil business, had given to the university a set of 10 residential units called colleges that came complete with dining halls, libraries and squash courts, a gift that amounted to $12 million. He did the about the same ($11,392,000 in 1930 dollars) for Harvard, where the units were called houses. Several of these buildings, with their narrow leaded windows, were and are Gothic…and thus somewhat gloomy.

The Old Howard was a revered burlesque house on Scollay Square in Boston, and the milk train was the night's last one out of Grand Central Terminal which made all 26 stops from Mount Vernon to New Haven, arriving there about 7 A.M. Rudy Vallee, the actor-singer; Peter Arno, the New Yorker magazine cartoonist; and Albie Booth, 1931 football captain, were all Yale men.

The Yale Bowl did hold Old Eli's gin. As a 12-year-old in 1936, after the Dartmouth game, I walked down the aisle to exit passing row after row of the linear premier seats on the Yale side, under which lay dozens of empties…pint bottles. The more mannerly flask and the football fete had coupled way back, within and beyond the Yale Bowl.

---

* By J. Brinkerhoff Jackson, Harvard '32, as performed in the Hasty Pudding Show of 1933 by James Dennison, Guy Hayes, Chester King, Kent Sanger and Lee Thurber, all 1934. Hasty Pudding Theatricals remains a traditional Harvard institution.

After that game a woman who had attended wrote the Yale president, James Rowland Angell, "In all our twenty years of attending football games we have never seen such a vulgar, revolting spectacle as last Saturday...Can nothing be done to stop this evil?"

President Harold Dodds of Princeton thought so. That same year he banned the consumption of alcohol in Palmer Stadium, saying, "Indulgence in alcoholic beverages at football games has assumed proportions which seriously menace the future of the sport as an intercollegiate activity." The *Daily Princetonian* approved, declaring, "We are proud of the fact that Princeton is willing to bear the thankless burden of the pioneer."

Yale did not comply.

That *Yalesmen must all become bond salesmen* struck a chord. Even after the crash of the stock market in October of 1929 and the resulting Great Depression, Wall Street had appeal to the many educated Elis who otherwise lacked particular skills or special ambitions. It was a pathway of small resistance and once in New York a Yale man would find many other Yale men of several past generations who could be helpful. Two of the Ironmen took that route after graduation, Choo Choo Train for one year and Kim Whitehead for five.

Those Harkness "colleges," seven of which had opened to undergraduate residency the previous autumn, made Yale in 1934 a nice place to be. The buildings, bare in their newness on a campus that had been a part of New Haven since 1718, replaced a hodgepodge of dormitories and rooming houses of the past. "New Yale" was a frequent reference.

The freshman class that fall...the Class of 1938...totaled 781, the lowest figure in 10 years and a significant seven per cent drop. The number of applications was down, a number left unannounced, and surely on account of the Depression. But Yale would not let "just anybody" through its doors, and 215 of the 781 had fathers who were Yale men.

The Dean of Freshmen, Percy T. Walden, '92 Sheff, made clear in his welcoming speech that the neophytes were on their own, as they had not been in boarding school or at home. "You decide your own conduct, whether to cut a class, whether to take a weekend in New York. You are your own boss."

The Ironmen…five seniors, three juniors and three sophomores…had heard the same in their freshman times.

In the new colleges the rates for a room, shared or a single, ranged from $110 to $400 per person for the two-term year. The student could subscribe for 21 meals in the dining halls per week for $8; 14 meals for $7, or 10 meals for $5.50, the last being the mandatory minimum.

Tuition was $450. So the big three…tuition, room & board (food)…owed the university averaged $1,000. The contemporary charge is 42 times that.

7

The Townie

All but one of the Ironmen lived in one of the new colleges, the exception being DeAngelis, the New Haven townie who did not have $1,000. Neither did Kelley. There were ways around the number.

Kelley was a waiter at the sports training tables...set up in a university house on Chapel Street not far from the campus...where steaks prevailed. As a football and baseball player as well as a table waiter he received his meals free. Also he had for three years a scholarship from an institution that looked after the football boys, the Yale Club of New York whose award likely took care of his tuition.

There was no hypocrisy here as to scholarship. Kelley throughout his Yale career was an honors student who just missed the level of Phi Beta Kappa at graduation in June, 1937. Six other Ironmen, Clare Curtin, DeAngelis, Jerry Roscoe, Meredith Scott, Jack Wright and Kim Whitehead, were also the recipients of various scholarships awarded for need, academic achievement or all-around virtue.

Stan Fuller

Meredith Scott

DeAngelis had been scrapping most of his life. His parents were Italian immigrants who "moved around a lot," said Jim. That was an euphemism for the city life common in an America that President Franklin Delano Roosevelt described as "one-third ill housed, one-third ill clad, one-third ill nourished."

As an enticement to rent their rooms, apartments or houses, landlords would advertise, "First month rent free." On the first the tenants would move in and on the 30th or 31st they would move out, repeating the scheme.

"I don't remember how we moved the furniture," said DeAngelis many, many years later. "But I know we moved."

When he was six years old, in 1917, DeAngelis found a benefactor, Clarence Blakeslee, who was the head of a large general contracting firm in New Haven, C.W. Blakeslee & Sons.

The advertisement in the Yale football programs declared the company to be builders of "Athletic fields, bridges, dams, foundations, roads, all heavy construction." At the time of their meeting the DeAngelis family lived across the street from the company headquarters on Waverly Street.

Clarence Blakeslee was a philanthropist like Edward S. Harkness, but on another scale. "He helped a lot of kids," said DeAngelis. "And never bragged about it. He loved kids. He'd take us for a ride in his car, all that kind of stuff. He took a liking to me for some reason and did a lot for me. He got me to join the YMCA; he sent me to summer camp."

Jim's father, when he had work, was a bricklayer, a stonemason, like countless other Italian immigrant men in the Northeast. His mother worked too, in the New Haven factories. "I never knew when she wasn't working," said DeAngelis, who had two sisters. "When I got out of grammar school I wanted to go to work to help support the family. She insisted I go to high school."

That was Hillhouse High, located then adjacent to the Yale campus. Chick Bowen was the football coach, and DeAngelis played center on the team for three seasons. After graduation in 1929 he found a job with Western Electric in Stamford, Conn., with no thought of college. "I was poor," he said emphatically long afterward. "My family didn't have a nickel."

One day Chick Bowen called. Richard (Pop) Lovell, a well-known New Haven Boys Club sports figure, was the new athletic director at Milford Prep, a private school 11 miles from New Haven that could polish a youth for entrance to college.

Albie Booth, the little Yale halfback of the 1929–1931 era whose darting runs brought thousands of adoring fans to the Yale Bowl, had gone from Hillhouse to Milford Prep and then to Yale. Booth was a hero to DeAngelis and just about every other New Haven youth.

Lovell, said Bowen, wanted Jim DeAngelis to come to Milford Prep. "I've got no money," said Jim. Bowen said, "Go see Mr. Blakeslee. He's a friend of yours."

DeAngelis did so. "Mr. Blakeslee told me, 'You go to school. Don't worry about your family. I'll see that they are taken care of.'

"And he did."

DeAngelis worked in the summers for the Blakeslee company. "I was a laborer," he said. "Pick and shovel. Push a wheelbarrow. Carry bags of cement. Whatever had to be done."

An Ironmen teammate, Kim Whitehead, also worked summers…in a different milieu. In 1934 he "tutored" or baby-sat the children of a prominent Cincinnati attorney, John B. Hollister, also a Yale man, at Nonquitt on Massachusetts' Buzzards Bay, where Whitehead enjoyed the tennis, the golf, the sailing and the beach clubs.

That fall the two of them backed up the Yale line on defense side-by-side. They were two tough cookies.

DeAngelis had entered Yale in the fall of 1931 with hopes of earning a civil engineering degree in the Sheffield Scientific School. So his class designation was 1935 Sheff or '35S. Yale for decades had been thus divided into Ac, or the academic course of study as in the Bachelor of Arts degree, and Sheff standing for the sciences.* Among the Ironmen, DeAngelis was the only Sheff man.

Jim DeAngelis

* In my father's time, 1911–1914, the Sheffield Scientific School awarded degrees after three years study rather than the normal four for Yale College. This seems to have been a dodge for some like Lew Wallace Jr. who were in a hurry to get through their formal education and who had no scientific bent whatsoever.

Jim lived at home his freshman year. "Mr. Blakeslee" had helped him buy the proper clothes, jackets, shirts and ties…not from the fancy shops on York Street, Langrocks or J. Press where the wealthy Yale lads had charge accounts, but rather at Malley's, everyone's downtown department store.

Booth looked out for his fellow Hillhouse townie. "From the other side of the tracks," as Jim described himself. Booth saw to it that DeAngelis joined his Sheff fraternity, St. Elmo, which had a big house on Grove Street across from Timothy Dwight College. DeAngelis lived there in his junior and senior years.

At St. Elmo there was a congenial climate, which Jim ignored. "They used to have the dances," he said. "I never went. I couldn't afford it. Social life was out for me."

He knew few classmates. "I didn't even get to know my teammates outside of football practice. They were all Ac and I was Sheff. Our paths didn't cross."

The DeAngelis contribution to the Ironmen game was crucial in five decisive plays. The first one came on the opening kickoff when he tackled Ken Sandbach at the Princeton one-yard line. In the second period this 165-pound linebacker stopped another Princeton halfback, Homer Spofford, at the Yale two. He made on-target center passes to Roscoe to set up the touchdown pass to Kelley, and those to Fuller for his two punts that went out of bounds on the Princeton two and three-yard lines in the fourth period.

Ken Sandbach

Jack Weller

He also survived an alleged Princeton assault on the Tigers' very first play from scrimmage. "Jack Weller tried to slug me," claimed DeAngelis. Weller was Princeton's all-America left guard. "That was Crisler. They wanted to get me out of the game early. Crisler knew how important the center was."

8

It Can Be Done

Besides DeAngelis the other seniors among the Ironmen were Clare Curtin, the captain and left guard; Stan Fuller, the left halfback for the moment; Ben Grosscup, the right guard; and Strat Morton, the right halfback.

Captain Francis Clare Curtin

After the fourth game, a loss to Army in which the Cadets ran over the Yale line, Curtin moved from right tackle to left guard to stiffen the middle and to bring a big sophomore, Jack Wright (6-1, 198), into the tackle position next to Kelley, his roommate in Trumbull College.

Most of Yale's plays were run from the single-wing formation with unbalanced line, a standard* for college teams in the two decades between the two World Wars, as was the 6-2-2-1 alignment of those players on defense. The unbalanced line went from left to right, as in right formation: end, guard, center, guard, tackle, tackle, end. The right guard would be the pulling one, to pull back from the scrimmage line and become the lead blocker on sweeps to the outside.

Ben Grosscup was best at that. Paul Benjamin Grosscup Jr. was from Charleston, W. Va., and his father had gone to Harvard. Choate had been his prep school and he was what might be nicely called a social jock: football, hockey and lacrosse in freshman year plus student council, prom and budget committees. He later joined the junior fraternity, Chi Psi, and was tapped (meaning chosen) for the Scroll and Key senior society. In addition he was predictably on those rugby teams that went to Bermuda and had such a good time during the spring vacations.

Although only 175 pounds, Grosscup had played center or guard for three seasons and was the scrappy kind of player that the line coach, Denny Myers, wanted on the field.

---

* A rule required the player throwing a pass to be at least five yards behind the line of scrimmage…imposed in 1910 and lasting to 1945…is why the contemporary T-formation, with the quarterback-passer right behind the center on the scrimmage line, was hardly ever seen.

Stan Fuller, the left halfback and the punter, was 25 years old, a year older than one of the assistant coaches, Ivy Williamson, and six years older than Larry Kelley. He came from Erie, Pennsylvania, and had spent a year at Ohio University before transferring to Yale. He had first sought admission from a prep school, Roxbury, but was refused on academic grounds. So he tried another route, by way of another college.

Football transfers had been somewhat common at Yale during the 1920's, the most famous being Century Milstead* from Wabash College, Mal Stevens from Washburn College, Widdy Neale from Marietta College and Bruce Caldwell from Brown.

Transfers were sometimes looked upon with disfavor by rivals...said to be *tramp athletes*...although Fuller, from Erie, Pa., was not the star-type athlete to cause jealousy or antipathy.

He was a steady spare backfield operator, sound on defense, a decent blocker who could also punt the football a bit better than Kim Whitehead and a lot better than anyone else Yale had. Therefore Neale, and Ducky Pond, had anointed him for a key role against the Tigers.

Bob Hall's voluminous scouting report had concluded, "Gary LeVan is their most dangerous weapon. Never let him get his hands on a kickoff or a punt."

As the practice week began Neale said, "Fuller, we're going to have you kick out of bounds whenever possible on Saturday. We've got to keep the ball away from LeVan. He's

---

* Milstead was born January 1, 1901, thus his given name. He, Neale (Greasy's brother), and Stevens (Yale's head coach, 1928–1932) were members of the undefeated 1923 team, one of Yale's finest.

dynamite. I want you to practice all week kicking out of bounds. And if you kick one to LeVan I'll take you right out."

Neale then placed a red flag at a 20-yard line and another on the goal line of the Anthony Thompson practice field, across Central Avenue from the Yale Bowl. Fuller practiced. And he did not disappoint.

Stratford Lee Morton Jr. was another steady, useful player that Neale counted upon for right halfback, the wingback spot in the single wing. The position required constant blocking for the other ball carriers and speed enough to earn yards on the reverses and occasionally catch a pass. Morton was in the starting lineup from the very first day at Gales Ferry.

Ben Grosscup

Strat Morton

Strat Morton came from St. Louis, or rather Clayton, the western suburb where the tony country clubs spread.* His father was a college man, Washington University of St. Louis, and Morton had attended the two private schools there, John Burroughs and St. Louis Country Day, before Yale.

His college credentials describe the handsome man: Fence Club fraternity, Scroll and Key senior society, captain of the rugby team. But he surprised his family and friends by enlisting in the Army Air Corps in June, 1939, and was commissioned as a second lieutenant the following May. He was killed on June 22, 1941, while piloting an A-20 bomber that flew into a Georgia swamp in a thunderstorm on a trip from Fort Benning to Chattanooga. This sudden death brought his classmates up short. Just 168 days before Pearl

* After Yale, Morton played polo for the St. Louis Country Club team.

Harbor some were anti-war isolationists and others oblivious or indifferent to the plight of Europe.

In their three varsity seasons these five seniors had played under three head coaches, Mal Stevens, Reg Root and now Ducky Pond, and after 21 varsity games the record was nine victories, nine losses, three ties. Yale, once a colossus of American football, had fallen upon hard times in keeping with the Depression.

The juniors were Roscoe, Train and Whitehead, quarterback, left end and fullback...a trio making up the core of the Ironmen.

Roscoe was the rare Californian at Yale, from San Diego, although his prep school had been Kent in Connecticut, 50 miles northwest of New Haven. He was the team's foremost passer, a decent runner and a sound safety man entrusted with the punt returns.

A rules change for 1934 further changed the shape of the football, reducing its belly circumference by one-half inch,* which made for a stronger grip and which further encouraged the forward pass and discouraged the drop kick. The fat ball was gone. "It made a big difference, I thought," said Roscoe 50 years later.

Train, the Georgian from Savannah, was a superb end for his era which required of the position strong defensive play and blocking, plus some pass-catching ability. Choo Choo

---

* In 1912 the football had a short circumference of 22 1/2 inches, meaning around the fat part. This was reduced to 22 inches in 1929 and 21 1/2 for 1934. The end-to-end circumference remained 29 inches. The ball continued to shrink by edict of the rules committees to its present short circumference...the important one...of 20 3/4 to 21 1/4 inches, and its long circumference of 27 3/4 to 28 1/2 inches.

came streaking across the field against Princeton to knock Gary LeVan out of bounds at the Yale 24 in the second period when the Tiger halfback seemed certain to reach the Yale goal.

Whitehead, from Westfield, N.J., was Yale's primary ball carrier at fullback and, with 165-pound DeAngelis, backed up the line on defense. He succeeded Curtin as captain for 1935.

And the sophomores were Kelley, Scott and Wright…right end, left tackle, right tackle.

Kelley did not start the season's first game, the loss to Columbia, and the coaches never made that mistake again. In his three varsity seasons Yale won 18 of its 25 games and Kelley scored points in all six Big Three matches against Harvard and Princeton, five of which were victories. That small feat has never been matched.

Choo Choo Train

Jack Wright

Scott and Wright were two useful 190-pound tackles who had been "discovered" at Gales Ferry. Scott, from a small prep school, Christchurch, and a small town, Gordonsville, in Virginia, became the starting left tackle by midseason. Wright, from Bronxville, N.Y., and Taft, was made the starter at right tackle before the Princeton game when Curtin was shifted to guard.

At last Pond and Neale had the team they wanted, the best eleven players sorting themselves into a combination that had not played as a unit before. The coaches had their scouting report and they knew what they had to do.

Their hunch? They had a chance.

Never mind that the Bulldogs had played indifferently in the 14-7 loss to Georgia the previous Saturday. After all, Roscoe had missed the game on account of a case of the grippe. Never mind that the practices during the week were grim and cold and that all the sportswriters had picked Princeton to win easily.

Hokus Berkman, the farceur in charge of the vast array of equipment that comes with a football team and who had caused generations of Yale players to laugh in the locker room, had put up a sign that read, "It Can Be Done." But the disposition of the players was hard to read. They were quiet for the most part.

Stanley Woodward of New York's *Herald Tribune*, a former Amherst tackle who wrote with authority and wit, stated in Saturday's paper, "Personally, I don't think Yale can win no matter what it does."

In a trip to New Haven on Thursday, Woodward was shut out from the closed practice but did write with insight, "The consensus seems to be that Yale's first team, if it does not suffer injuries, will be able to play Princeton even. Everyone admits, however, that Princeton has a great advantage in reserve manpower and will gain an edge with every substitution."

9

Princeton's Coincidentals

It did not occur to Woodward, nor anyone else, that that there would be no substitutions for Yale. Ironmen games were as rare as comets. In the so-called modern era, meaning the seasons following World War I, there had been only three in all of college football.

Michigan and Illinois in 1925 had both played for 60 minutes at Ann Arbor, Mich., in rain and mud without either team offering a substitute. The final score was 3-0 for the Wolverines and Red Grange of the Illini had been stopped cold.* The next season Brown, with Tuss McLaughry as the new coach, sent out eleven men on two successive Saturdays. They beat Yale, 7-0, and Dartmouth, 10-0, without relief thus earning their nickname, Ironmen. They were unbeaten too but tied Colgate in their 10th and final contest.

After the Yale feat there were no more Ironmen games in college football ever, a claim based on an extensive search by the author.

---

* Fielding Yost, the Michigan coach, said, "Grange didn't gain enough ground to bury him in…even if they buried him head down." The season before Grange had scored five touchdowns against Michigan.

Was this a remarkable deed of endurance? That would depend upon the relativity. Counting the kickoffs (5) and the punts (24), there were 138 plays in the Princeton-Yale contest evenly divided as to offense and defense for each side and typical of a close game in that era.

Surviving 138 football plays was hardly comparable to the continuous action of a basketball game, a marathon or climbing Mt. Everest. Yet it was something and those 11 Bulldogs were exhausted when they finished, as we shall find out.

In contemporary "two-platoon" offense-defense football, no player is ever exhausted unless badly out of shape. A play consumes only 3-4-5 seconds and running backs, wide receivers plus some defensive specialists come in for one play and then go to the sideline again. Bursts of energy are required, not so much endurance.

In those olden times the participants sometimes "took a play off," meaning they didn't give their absolute all on every single play. That was hardly a secret. They were pacing themselves, saving themselves for the fourth quarter.

Let us say that the achievement of the Ironmen had more merit than flag-pole sitting, a popular avocation of the 1930's.

Princeton indeed had reserves. Coach Crisler's first successful recruiting year brought a harvest of, it was said, 30 prep school captains for the freshman class of 1933, meaning the graduating class of 1937. When asked how this came about, Crisler had a pat answer. He said it was merely a coincidence that these captains all showed up at Old Nassau.

After that explanation some writers with a touch of whimsy, such as Len Elliott of the Newark *Evening News*, referred to those Tigers as "the coincidentals."

The Princeton ends were Gil Lea, 6-2, 170, and Hugh MacMillan, 6-1, 170, both juniors. MacMillan, a former halfback, was the punter and occasionally wound up carrying the ball on trick plays or at the end of laterals. He was an Exeter product, from Cumberland, Md.

Lea might have been tiger striped from birth. His father was the celebrated Langdon (Biffy) Lea, a Princeton all-America of 1894 who later coached at Princeton, Michigan and elsewhere and who raised his sons to play this game as he had…all out, all the time. Gil Lea, from Wynnewood, Pa., had come to Princeton from the St. Paul's School of New Hampshire.

The left tackle was Gil Stoess, a 21-year-old sophomore from Atlantic City who got to the university through the back door of Princeton Prep. Another preparatory school in the town of Princeton, The Hun School,* had polished Jack Weller, the all-America left guard from Jacksonville, Fla., a 200-pound junior. The right guard was Dick John, a senior from Valley Forge Military Academy and Pottstown, Pa., and the right tackle David Chamberlain, a senior from Great Neck, Long Island, who had gone to the "Yale" prep school, Hotchkiss in Lakeville, Conn.

The captain and center, Elwood (Mose) Kalbaugh, and the quarterback, John (Kats) Kadlic, both came from Bellaire in the Ohio River football country near Martin's Ferry and Steubenville, and they prepped at Kiski, the renowned Pennsylvania football foundry. The blond Kadlic was just 5 feet 8 and 155 pounds, but like steel.

---

* Those two, sometimes called "tutoring schools," majored in preparing average students for Princeton admission. The Yale equivalents were Cheshire Academy, Milford Prep and The Roxbury School.

Captain Elwood Kalbaugh

Crisler had backs galore, the regulars besides Kadlic being junior fullback Pepper Constable, from Baltimore and the Gilman prep school there; sophomore Ken Sandbach, from Hun and Maplewood, N.J., and junior Garrett B. LeVan Jr., from Steubenville to Princeton by way of the Lawrenceville school.

LeVan, 5-9, 153 pounds, of course was the ace. Lou Little, the Columbia coach, said of him (to George Trevor of the New York *Sun*), "He has every trick of the broken field runner's trade, the pivot, the cross-step, hip-swivel, duck, change of pace, straight arm, abrupt stop, spin and speed burst. He thinks two tacklers ahead."

Trevor put further fear in the minds of Yale men by writing that LeVan could be as elusive as Albie Booth (5 feet 7, 144 pounds) had been for the Bulldogs just a few seasons earlier but was also "much faster and far stronger."

The additional Tiger backs included Spofford, who had been injured most of the season but was fit for the Bulldogs, Les Kaufman from West Haven, Conn., practically next door to the Yale Bowl, Paul Pauk from Branford, Conn., just east of New Haven, and Sumner (Ippy) Rulon-Miller Jr., from an eminent Princeton-Philadelphia Main Line family.

What other advantages did the Princeton team have over Yale in addition to its winning streak and its coincidentals? Not size. The two teams were even when it came to scale and smaller, say, than Notre Dame. Princeton's starting seven linemen averaged 6-0, 181 pounds; Yale's 6-0, 186 (the edge being Curtin's heft at 225). The single-wing backfield averages were 5-10, 168 for Princeton and 5-11, 167 for Yale. Notre Dame, which won six of nine games that season, averaged 6-0, 191 in the line, 6-0 and 188 in its backfield.

One might point out that Matt Birk, the admirable tackle of Harvard's Ivy League champions of 1997, weighed 312 pounds by 2000 as an all-star center for the Minnesota Vikings of the National Football League. That is almost *twice* as much as the Yale center of 1934, Jim DeAngelis.

More as to numbers: Pat Garvan went out and got 5-to-1 odds* on Yale to win from New Haven bookies, who could be found in the blocks between Chapel, Church, College and Crown Streets off The Green. He could afford to lose his wagers.

Francis (Pat) Garvan Jr. was the attractive blond manager of Yale's football team, a position of some prestige whose

---

* According to sources. Point lines were rare in those days but Stanley Woodward wrote that Princeton was a 13-point favorite. He may have made that up.

primary purpose was to make the travel arrangements when the Yale squad went out of town.

That was seldom. Because Yale Bowl was so capacious other teams came there, like Brown 51 times between 1904 and 1957 and Dartmouth 46 times between 1924 and 1970...only to lose two times out of three.

Pat Garvan had style, class and money, New York money. His father, an 1897 Yale graduate, was a lawyer who had been appointed the alien property custodian after World War I which meant he was in charge of the German chemical patents assigned to the United States. From that he helped to organize the American chemical industry.

He and his wife, Mabel Brady Garvan, were formidable collectors of American decorative art majoring in furniture and silver. Yale and the Metropolitan Museum in New York were beneficiaries, Garvan giving to the university in 1930 some 5,000 objects in honor of his wife. Over the decades, the Garvans' gifts and bequests came to number close to 10,000 works of American paintings, prints, sculpture and decorative arts.

And the son, as it turned out, had those New Haven pursers at his mercy as did Bob Cooke and Lou Walker, the plungers who had flown to Detroit to wager on the seventh game of the World Series. Walker was the manager of the lightweight 150-pound varsity team and the roommate of Roscoe in the new Berkeley College. He had "a feeling" about the upcoming match.

And he would be on the train tomorrow.

10

Redemption or Regret?

When Friday, November 16, came around Pat Garvan had the arrangements completed and the Yale itinerary printed in two colors, black and red, on a tidy six-sided 3" by 6" cardboard fold-out for all the participants.

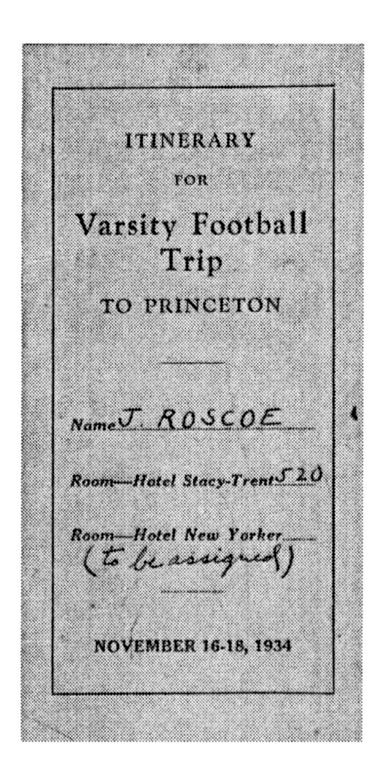

ITINERARY

FOR

Varsity Football Trip

TO PRINCETON

Name J. ROSCOE

Room—Hotel Stacy-Trent 520

Room—Hotel New Yorker (to be assigned)

NOVEMBER 16-18, 1934

PRINCETON TRIP
NOVEMBER 16–18, 1934

DRINK ONLY SPECIAL WATER
AT ALL TIMES

Friday, November 16

9:20 A.M.—Bring own bag to bus outside Yale Station. Be sure to have special baggage tag on it.

Yale Station was the post office in the basement of Wright Hall on Elm Street and a campus focal point. To the surprise of the athletes a significant segment of the 76-piece Yale Band had assembled there to provide a gala send-off, one featuring the inimitable "Boola Boola." And the perpetual favorite: "Good-Night, Poor Princeton."

It was an unrehearsed effort that attracted maybe a hundred students who clapped and cheered. There had been a stirring of enthusiasm about the campus during the week, the persuasion of football sparkle that had been absent since the heady days of Albie Booth came to a close three years before.

10:00 A.M.—Train No. 7 leaves New Haven Station. Two Pullmans are reserved for the Varsity Squad. These same Varsity cars go through to Princeton. Luncheon on train. Every one to sign his own check personally.

There were 65 in the Yale party by Garvan's count, 28 of whom were the players. After the three-and one-half-hour train trip right into the rail yard adjacent to the Princeton campus, those 28 walked to the McCormick Field House and put on the football gear taken from Berkman's trunks. Then came a 90-minute practice within Palmer Stadium, where counsel said they were to be shredded the next afternoon.

On autumnal Friday afternoons the empty coliseums like Palmer, with the lifeless cement seating above, can be intimidating for the stopover team. It was said the Yale workout seemed flat, bumbling.

4:00 P.M.—Squad goes to Hotel Stacy-Trent by bus.

The Stacy-Trent Hotel, close to Trenton's Pennsylvania Railroad station, was an agreeable commercial hotel then in an agreeable city of 48,000 population, the state capital nine miles south of Princeton. The Yale party took up 48 rooms and Coach Pond and his wife had the penthouse suite on the tenth floor.

Each occupant found in his room the makings of a still life painting…one apple and one bottle of water, Chippewa brand. Yale could not trust that Jersey water, from the Delaware River visible out the windows.

Those graces were the doing of Major Frank Wandle, the team trainer who along with Pond's coaching staff represented the New Deal for Yale football.

Wandle had come to Yale from the Military Academy, West Point, and he had done a lot of good. A retired military person Wandle knew much about diet as well as physiology and thus was unlike anyone Yale football had experienced before.

Training Rules and Hints, a modest little booklet, had come out that fall with the authorship and authority only of the Yale University Athletic Association. Page one: no smoking, no drinking, no "late hours." Dismissal, etc.

Pat Garvan

But everyone knew it was the work of The Major on account of its inclusiveness and the penetrating aphorisms.

"Of course you will feel nervous before a contest. If you weren't you wouldn't be much good to your team. Ever notice a horse champing on his bit or pawing the ground? If it effects *(sic)* a dumb animal, it's natural for a human to feel this way. As soon as the starting whistle blows your nervousness will disappear.

"Of course there will be days of Sunshine and days of Darkness. They are your 'ups and downs.' We all have them. Think of the bright side of life. Tomorrow the Sun will be shining again."

Saturday, November 17

9:15 A.M.—Probably a board talk in dining room. Everybody must get bandaged by the Major in his room, No. 505.

12:00 Noon—Team will leave for McCormick Field House by bus. Personal baggage will be taken care of during game.

The half hour ride was a silent one but there was a mood that the team captain, Clare Curtin, attempted to describe years later. He said, "We were fed up with all the ballyhoo about this big Princeton team of destiny. It was a personal, individual thing that most of us felt…to heck with this big team. We're going to knock them off."

A silent boast? More likely Curtin was expressing a certain earthiness that had often been a part of Yale football. Previous captains like Frank Hinkey (1893 and 1894), Tom Shevlin (1905), Cupe Black (1916) and Fay Vincent (1930) were tough operators. In the early years of this sport a lot of blood was left on the field when Yale teams played.

The deal at Palmer Stadium on game day came in two parts. The first part took place in the field house. where the players dressed, not far from the stadium. They pulled on those scratchy wool jerseys over the shoulder pads and the "canvas" pants that came with a built-in hip pad.

Numbers? Yes, on the back of the jerseys. There was no system. Yale's went from 14 to 55 indiscriminately as to position. Princeton took up almost every number from 22 through to 99, the last for the best player, Jack Weller.

Helmets? These leather models by Spalding were well made, with an inside protective crown. They could be painted. Yale's were white which made sense contrasting with the Yale-blue[*] jersey and the standard beige pants below which came blue knee-socks.

The Princeton helmet, from the same source, sent a message that reverberates to this day. Spalding affixed as a binder to secure all the elements a leather patch in the front of the helmet, just above the brow. Behind that there came three separate strip bindings from front to back.

Crisler chose to have those bindings painted orange and the body of the helmet black. The effect was orange wings of a sort. When he left Princeton in 1938 Crisler took the design to Michigan, where maize replaced the orange and blue the black. The pattern survives to this day, an affectation on the hard plastic shell of the contemporary helmet. Crisler coaching progeny took the design to places like Delaware and Maine, while Princeton abandoned the motif for a few decades and then brought it back.

The next part of game day at Princeton centered upon a secondary "squad" room, a small enclave beneath the stadium structure in its under parts. There were two such rooms, one for Princeton, one for the opponent, to be used for pregame assembly and halftime rest, consultation.

By noonday Lew Wallace Jr. and son Billy were not exactly whizzing down Route 1 through New Brunswick and on to Princeton. Stoplight, stoplight, stoplight. But it was a glorious day, so warm. Like summer.

The last time Yale had been to Princeton, 1932, the game had ended in an unsatisfactory 7-7 tie between two accursed teams. That damn dressing room underneath the stadium had

---

[*] Yale blue has had its variations. In this period it was cobalt blue, a deep but not dark blue.

been damn cold, complained Mal Stevens, the coach.* The small wood stove therein was unlit.

This time Princeton would be more cordial. The wood stove was stoked and the little room "hotter than hell," said Jim DeAngelis. "It must have been 110 in there. Ducky was ranting and raving for someone to break open the windows."

The Yale team needed the space for the collective equipment checks with Hokus and the last words from the coaches. It was said that the windows had been nailed shut and Crisler was given the blame, of course. The Bulldogs were distrusting about anything pertaining to the Princeton coach.

Pond did not have anything inspiring to say. That was not his style. But Crisler was an orator in the Knute Rockne fashion.

"Gentlemen, I have not the honor to be a Princeton man, so I do not feel that I can intrude myself upon the sanctity of this moment. I leave you with your own thoughts. It is your choice to make. What is it to be? Sixty minutes of redemption or a lifetime of regret?"

Wow. No wonder the Tigers were wound tight. What was it they were supposed to redeem? Their coach did not specify.

Perhaps he had in mind the game of three years before, won by Yale, 51-14, the most decisive margin in the history of the rivalry. But Crisler was at Minnesota then and none of the current players had participated.

---

* Because of economies due to the Depression each team played only seven games that fall. Princeton won 2, lost 2, tied 3. So did Yale exactly. The two played in three 0-0 games, Yale's against Bates being unacceptable for Old Blues who became increasingly critical of Stevens, their coach. He quit at season's end.

No, he wasn't a Princeton man, but he owed his career to a Yale man. Crisler grew up on a farm near Earlville, Ill., 70 miles west of Chicago. The high school had only 15 boys and all played football except for two, a cripple and Crisler. He was six feet tall but weighed only 100 pounds.

He earned an academic scholarship to the University of Chicago, whose football coach was the small but dynamic Amos Alonzo Stagg. Stagg's long association with the sport had begun at Yale as an undergraduate and graduate student, 1884 to 1889, playing for Walter Camp, the "father of football."*

Herbert Crisler went out for football at Chicago as a freshman and quit at the end of the first day. He returned after Stagg said to him, "I never thought you'd be a quitter."

His progress was slow. After he butchered the same play several times in practice, Stagg told Crisler about a famous violinist, Fritz Kreisler, who 'has genius, skill and coordination and knows how to use them," said the coach. "From now on I'm going to call you Fritz too, just to remind myself that you are absolutely his opposite."

Crisler, who went on to win nine varsity letters in football, basketball and baseball, revered Stagg and after graduation in 1922, having abandoned the idea of a medical career, he became the latter's assistant for eight seasons. Stagg continued to call him Fritz and so did everyone else.**

---

* Head coach at Springfield, 1890–91; Chicago, 1892–1933; College of Pacific, 1933–1946; co-head coach with his son, Susquehanna, 1947–1952. Stagg died in 1965 at the age of 102.

** The coach and the violinist met during a concert at Ann Arbor and Kreisler asked what he could play for Crisler. "Danny Boy" was the reply.

The new coach liked Princeton. Midway through his second season—which would be an undefeated season—he replied to a question in an interview printed in the Yale *Daily News* (and clipped by Roscoe), "Oh, I'm much happier here. The men are a finer type, pick things up more quickly, and besides are well grounded in the game when they get to me. In universities such as Minnesota and Michigan, if they have more brawn, it's because they have eleven or twelve thousand from which to pick. Five hundred men turn out for football."

To get rid of this pesky Yale team, the Princeton coach had set up a blocking scheme for the start, presuming the Tigers would receive the opening kickoff.

Gil Lea explained in an interview 70 years later. "The plan was to score on the kickoff," he said. "Throw them off balance, get the momentum going and run up the score before they knew what hit them."

It made sense as Princeton had scored six touchdowns on kickoffs that season by massing the blocking to the right and opening an avenue up the sideline for the returner. But this time the Tigers would set the blocking lane to the left, knowing that Yale scouts had tracked their every move all season.

The two universities had promised not to spy on one another several years before but this non-scouting agreement had run out after 1933. So Bob Hall and his spies were in the stands at every Princeton game with binoculars and note books. Play-by-play films of the games existed but they had not yet come into use as a scouting tool.

The captains, Clare Curtin and Mose Kalbaugh, met at midfield for the coin toss which went to Yale. The Elis elected to kick off, following the Greasy Neale strategy of letting the other team handle the ball in the early settling-down phase.

Curtin, who had a strong leg, booted the ball out of bounds and the rules required a repeat. His second kick went into the Princeton end zone where Ken Sandbach caught the ball and dropped it. He picked it up, juggled it, and then decided to exit the end zone, to take advantage of the blocking lane the coaches said would be there.

His was a terrible decision. Here came the Yale men. At the one yard line he was met by DeAngelis, who tackled him there.

The jittery Tigers, concerned about redemption and regret, did not need a blunder at the game's birth. If Sandbach, a sophomore, had merely touched the ball down in his end zone it would have been a touchback and Princeton would have had possession and a first down at its 20 yard line. Not at its one.

"We lost the game right there," said Lea, with considerable hindsight.

11

Does The Rose Bowl Have Handles?

Frank D. Halsey, Princeton Class of 1912, wrote game accounts for the *Alumni Weekly*—astute, penetrating and honest accounts. He was merciless regarding the defeat by Yale in which he started out Biblically: "Tell it not in Gath, publish it not in the streets of Askalon, and see *2 Samuel 1 :19.* In short Yale upset our apple cart, and what rejoicing there may be in the camp of our enemies is fully justified."

Warming to his mission, Halsey went on, "Yale consistently made the most of what it had; we made practically no intelligent use of what we were supposed to have and were sloppy and erratic to boot. Therein, I think, lies what explanation there may be of a result which practically defies explanation.

"This admission that, although we were undoubtedly superior in man-power we were inferior in intelligence and poise, is a sad one to have to make. But I do not see what else there is to say or how it can be kept a secret."

The writer next misidentified the Princeton player who botched the opening kickoff return, blaming LeVan when it was Sandbach. He made no other errors, however.

Princeton immediately punted on first down, reflecting the kind of thinking of the time: Get the ball out of there. Don't run the risk of a mistake so close to one's own goal. Let the opponent make the offensive mistakes.

LeVan punted 50 yards out of his end zone to the Tiger 40 where Roscoe made the first of his eight punt returns, gaining 10 yards. Wrote Robert Kelley in the New York *Times*, "Then a five-yard offside penalty against Princeton gave the crowd, right at the outset, the altogether surprising sight of Yale attacking from the Princeton 25-yard line."

The Yale opportunity ended six plays later when Roscoe's pass was intercepted by linebacker Mose Kalbaugh who returned 24 yards to the Yale 48. "Had he been as fast a man as LeVan it would have been an easy touchdown," wrote Halsey.

On Princeton's second offensive play Pepper Constable fumbled and linebacker Whitehead recovered for Yale. Two plays gained two yards and Roscoe called for a third-down punt, as Neale had taught him in such a situation. Stan Fuller made the first of his 13 punts for Yale, a big one that went into the Princeton end zone for a touchback.

Next another punt for Princeton followed by one more from Fuller for Yale, also into the end zone for a touchback. LeVan on first down fumbled but recovered…Princeton's second of eight fumbles…and his third-down punt, partially blocked, went high and just 20 yards. Strat Morton had a return of two to the Princeton 46 with three minutes left to play in the first period. Morton gained three and then lost six when Gil Lea trapped him.

Roscoe described what next took place. "We had practiced the fake-punt-and-pass often but never used it," he said. "Even though it was 3rd down I thought Princeton would take the bait, and when we went into kick formation their two corner backs *(Kadlic and Sandbach)* dropped further back than normal to block for LeVan leaving a hole in the middle, just as it was drawn on X and O charts.

"We were in our standard punt formation with Fuller back to punt. Whitehead was to the left and I to the right of the pass-back lane, in tandem about 5 yds. back of the scrimmage line and Morton was lined up just off Kelley's rear. A lineman pulled right to protect when both Kelley and Morton took off down field, and Whitehead covered when Train took off.

"The ball was snapped by DeAngelis directly to me, and I dropped straight back. Fuller went through a full fake punt and then went forward to block for me if needed. Train on the left went down about 10 yds. and out, Morton the same on the right, and Kelley after going down slightly rightish about 15 yds. cut left and downfield and was wide open in the middle.

"I suspect neither LeVan or his two deep blockers saw the ball when it was snapped to me and did take Fuller's fake and stayed back until too late.*

"In practice the ball was always thrown high on this play to protect against an interception and a high pass was made possible by Kelley's ability to go up high and use his hands so well.

"This wasn't the prettiest pass I ever threw…the spiral wasn't perfect and it was a little higher than intended. But Kelley jumped high at the 25 yd. line, extended his right arm up and trapped the ball with his right hand…grabbed it and was off, faking 3 Princetonians out of their shoes enroute!"

There were many versions of Kelley's remarkable run to the goal and no replay from television to sort them out. A news photograph taken from the roof of Palmer Stadium's press box showed Kelley amid five Tigers when he made the catch. Train managed to screen off Kadlic momentarily as

* Constable always said, according to his wife Betty, that he never saw the football on the play until it rested in Kelley's arms.

Kelley cut behind his teammate heading for the sideline. Two others, Sandbach and LeVan, barred the way to the end zone.

L. to R. Sandbach and Kadlic, Train, Kelley, Constable, Kalbaugh

Stanley Woodward, in the *Herald Tribune*, wrote, "He *(Kelley)* snared the ball with a brilliant jumping catch, then pivoted and ran for the Yale sideline. He appeared to be cornered when he reached the 10-yard line then slowed down and bulleted *(sic)* for the end zone as three Princeton men missed him."

Robert Kelley's version, in the *Times*, was that Kelley "half-twisted, half-turned through these two *(sic)* men as though he were a ghost to cross the line standing up and unscathed."

Preferred is Roscoe's version, even though recorded 50 years later. "Kelley was going mostly right to left when he caught the ball and kept going that way for a few strides, and turning down field. The two Princeton backs *(LeVan and Sandbach)* were also going right to left when Kelley approached and it was that fact which made it possible for him to make that marvelous stop, dead in his tracks, and then continue on for the touchdown. The sideline did not force Kelley's stop. He did it because they were going too fast, and he was smart enough not to try to plow through them."

Kelley's explanation was simplistic. "Now I see these two guys coming at me. So I just stop dead and they slide right by me and I walk over the goal line."

Roscoe had a postscript. "Larry had large strides which tended to make him look as though he wasn't running especially fast. He was easily the fastest man on our squad. In the practice 50 yd. sprints he'd go along even with our fastest players, and then at 40 yds. take off and win easily.

"On numerous occasions in the two years I passed to him, I knew he could jack up his 90 % speed to 100 % and get the ball. It fooled a lot of defensive backs."

The Yale stands had come alive while Princeton stalwarts were mute. Clare Curtin kicked the extra point and Yale had a seven-point lead. Of course it would not last.

Sandbach this time successfully returned Curtin's kickoff out to the Princeton 28-yard line. But on second down LeVan fumbled again and Fuller recovered for Yale at the Tiger 33. Perhaps it was at this moment…or during the ensuing time-out when the quarter ended…that Ben Grosscup said loud enough for his subjects to hear, "Hey, Kadlic. Does the Rose Bowl have handles on it?" That was a neat needle.

The Bulldogs had another chance. But they could not advance and Fuller punted over the goal again. The first period came to an end.

The Tigers seemed frustrated and the Yales listened as they bickered. "We could hear a lot of talking in the Princeton huddle," recalled Roscoe. "The constant and challenging chatter by Grosscup, DeAngelis and Kelley couldn't have helped them much. It went on the whole game."

Grosscup, who played left guard on defense over Frank John or in the gap between John and the Princeton center, Kalbaugh, had come up with something better than a wise-crack. He said, "I saw that Kalbaugh had a habit of dragging the ball an inch or two along the ground before he snapped it. So I told our guys to back up a little off the line and when he started inching it, take off. We were in their backfield all afternoon."

Not quite. Late in the second quarter LeVan broke loose over right tackle and cut back for the sideline. Away he went. Choo Choo Train, Yale's left end, saw it this way: "The play started toward me. He *(LeVan)* cut back inside tackle behind Kelley and Morton and was off down the sideline. I had been taught never to quit chasing a play. When he busted open I was about parallel to him and put on a burst of speed and I got him."

Train rolled LeVan out of bounds 24 yards short of the Yale goal. LeVan completed a pass—one of only two orange & black completions—to Hugh MacMillan and Roscoe, the safety, forced him out of bounds at the Yale five. That set up a goal-line stand by the Bulldogs with the crowd in an uproar.

LeVan tried the middle of the Yale line and gained nothing. Spofford, the formerly injured star now in the contest, ran left to the two where DeAngelis, the lightweight linebacker, threw him down to save a score.

It was Constable's turn. The 185-pound fullback smashed at the Blue line but Grosscup stopped him cold. No gain. Spofford tried again on fourth down and Grosscup, getting a jump, nailed him for a one-yard loss.

The Elis took over at their three. Fuller's one poor punt, a hurried one, went only to the Yale 30 but Train chased Spofford, the returner, back for a six-yard loss. Princeton made a first down at the Elis' 23 and attempted three passes from there, all incomplete. The first half was over.

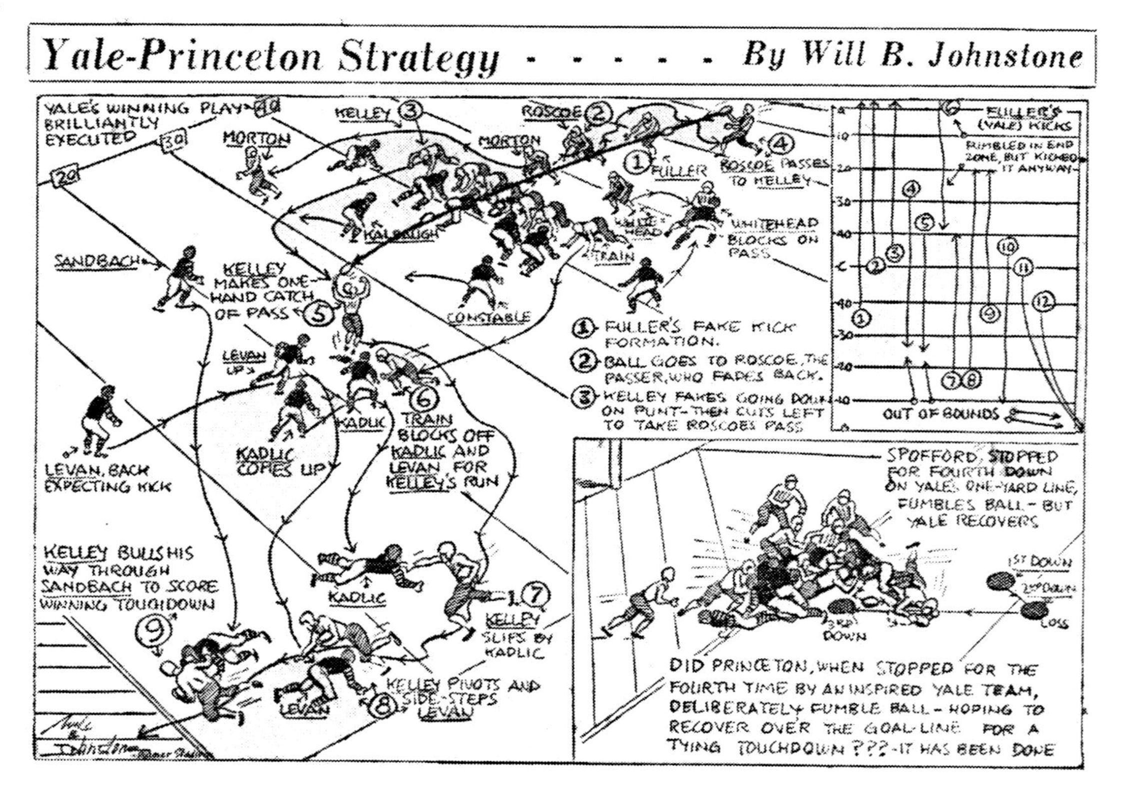

An accurate, well-done cartoon-diagram from Newark Evening News

12

Let Eleven Men Beat Them

Major Wandle, the trainer, had a blind spot. He was leery of water for his athletes and did not proffer it in the halftime room, that hot box under the stands. Instead he had Lou Walker, the assistant manager, soak sugar cubes with a handy bottle of rum and hand them out. "They tasted terrible," DeAngelis remembered.

Whitehead had been hit from the side on a kickoff play, a knee buckled and the Major attended him. "I think he gave me a pain killer," said Whitehead afterward. "He told me to get up and try it a little longer. So I tried it a little longer and longer until the game was over."

Crisler had a problem but there was little he could do other than voice the predictable. Settle down and play the type of ball you're capable...You can beat these guys...Hold on to the ball!

There was the usual milling around of the crowd inside and outside the stadium during the halftime break. Seventy years later I cannot say what Billy Wallace and his father did during those minutes. I like to believe we were both elated and fearful. For this was one of those games of intense anticipation—like an emerging no-hitter in baseball. Wait, wait, wait for something to happen, trusting it will be good...Yale holds…yet apprehensive it will be bad…Princeton takes command. We were to wait, one play at a time.

An interminable 30 minutes of combat remained for the not-yet christened ironmen. Fuller's punts saved them.

The first of seven in the second half went 70 yards from the point of the kick, rolling to a stop at Princeton's 28. From there the Tigers swept to first downs at their 45, at the Yale 37 on a 17-yard sweep around Kelley's end by LeVan, and at the Yale 12 following Constable's 21-yard end run to the other side. Another goal-line stand was at hand and we all stood up.

Gary LeVan

Kats Kadlic

The blocking formed for LeVan to hit at right end and he gained five yards before Train stopped him. That was oh, so close. Kaufman added two more. But on third down Kadlic called for passes, having decided the Yale line was too tough to crack for the last five yards. Then LeVan's pass into the end zone was almost intercepted by Fuller.

On fourth down Kadlic dropped to pass to an open MacMillan deep in the end zone. He caught the ball and the Princeton crowd gasped. Touchdown?

No. MacMillan's foot was on the end line, out of bounds. An official waved off the completion and Yale had a touchback, the ball going to the Bulldogs at their 20-yard line. Another wave of relief swept through the Yale sections of Palmer Stadium.

Fuller's next punt became Greasy Neale's inexcusable act. It went to LeVan on the run and the Princeton speedster aimed for the sideline with Train in pursuit once more. He had an angle.

Used Ticket stub, Yale side, Student Rate $2.20.

The Choo Choo man from Savannah later said, "I thought he was going to step out of bounds. And I was going to give him a good lick in the process. I didn't hold back and he was still running and I hit him and we went flying across the Yale bench and took the head linesman with us.

"LeVan caught his ribs on the bench and was laying there on the ground. I thought he was dead."

This was at the Yale 44.

"I said to Whitehead, 'The guy's hurt. And I did it.'

"And ole Happy says, 'I wish you'd killed the sonofoabitch.'"

Train had taken a good lick himself. Ducky Pond looked him over and said, "We better get him out of there."

"Let him go," said Greasy Neale. "The hell with it. Let eleven men beat them."

That was the first and only mention of an endurance contest, an ironman feat.

LeVan got up and walked across to the Princeton side to the applause of the big crowd on its collective feet once more. Paul Pauk came out to replace him. Another exchange of punts followed with Fuller sending out a rocket of 62 yards to Nassau's 24 where Pauk was buried by Bulldogs.

"In the middle of the third quarter," wrote Roscoe, "MacMillan got off a huge spiraling high punt, one of those kind that turn over in flight and add many yards to the length of the kick. As it came down I could see a Princeton lineman coming very fast, which is often a no-no because one step will dodge them *(sic)*.

"But I misjudged and just as I caught the ball his helmet hit me square in the face. That's all I remember until Frank Wandle's smelling salts under my nose woke me up. Fortunately my head cleared in a short time and I was able to stay in the game.

"We didn't wear a face mask of any sort in those days and his helmet hit on the left side of my face kind of between my eyebrow, cheek and nose. Nothing broken but before the game was over they were swollen and very sore.

"I was knocked over backward, flat on my back, but somehow held on to the ball. Perhaps some instinct involved, but more likely just plain luck…on our 20 yd. line!"

One more punting swap followed and this time Fuller aimed for the sideline. His kick went out of bounds on the Princeton 22.

Roscoe added: "Shortly after I was knocked flat catching a punt about in the middle of the third period, Fuller kicked well into Princeton territory, and from then until game end they never had possession of the ball on offense in our territory.

"The Yale line and linebackers hit harder throughout the game than I had thought possible, and in the end it was the Princeton line that was outplayed.

"On one play Whitehead hit LeVan so hard than when he started to get up his eyes were not focusing. He just had a blank look.

"Many years later we were discussing the game and he brought up that hit, and said he didn't remember anything until several plays later. That sort of thing is not unusual in football but I've never forgotten it in quite that way."

So the Tigers were stymied once more and the third quarter ended with Yale at the Princeton 38 following a 10-yard pass from Roscoe to Kelley.

Another Roscoe-Kelley completion gained 10 more and the Yale was at the Princeton 23. Roscoe called for Curtin to try a field goal of 40 yards, one that went wide of the goal posts at the back of the end zone, and Princeton took over at its 20.

"As the 4th quarter wore on," Roscoe wrote, "and Fuller kept putting them into a deep hole, Princeton kept on punting back, including twice on 1st down with their kicker behind their goal line. Before the first of these punts I suddenly hard a loud, '*Drop It Roscoe*.'

"The voice sounded very near. I glanced over at the Princeton side and saw an old and good friend I had gone to school with at Kent, Bish Colmore,* sitting there in his white cheerleader sweater and pants with a large megaphone to his mouth.

---

* His father was the Episcopal Bishop of Puerto Rico.

"I gave him a 'one-up' sign and thereafter I got the same but louder…*'Drop It Roscoe'*…frequently for the rest of the game. I didn't find it distracting and if anything I was damned determined that I wasn't going to drop a punt."

The home throng grew uneasy as the clock droned on. MacMillan, the end, tried a pass on a trick play. But Fuller intercepted, the fourth turnover for the Tigers. Playing carefully now, Yale on fourth down had Fuller punt once more and this time he accomplished what the vernacular called a coffin-corner kick…one that went out of bounds at the Princeton two-yard line to help seal the coffin.

Hugh MacMillan

Gil Lea

MacMillan punted right back on first down; Yale failed to make a first down and Fuller punted again to the coffin-corner, this time the ball going out of bounds at the Tiger three. Once more Old Nassau kicked to Roscoe who returned 20 yards to the foe's 25. An unnecessary roughness penalty placed Yale on the Tiger 10. Three plays gained three yards and Roscoe called for Curtin to try another field goal, one of only 25 yards. It just missed, high enough, far enough, wide.

Neale later scolded his field general. "He thought I should never have tried the 2nd field goal," wrote Roscoe. "Too much risk of a blocked kick. I was confident with Curtin's kicking ability and wanted to put the game away, end the uncertainty. For years Greasy and I used to discuss the two viewpoints. Since then I've come to agree, too much risk at game end when we were holding them well."

Princeton was all but done. On first down at its 20, Sandbach tried a pass which Fuller knocked down. He tried another and Whitehead intercepted at the 32 returning to the 28.

"There came a time towards the end of the game when our doubts began to recede," Roscoe recalled. "We could see and hear their frustration. But we had gone through two examples of how explosive they could be, and if any one of us sounded cocky he got a quick reminder to double up the pressure.

"I don't think any one of us believed until Whitehead intercepted that final pass on their 28, leaving us only one play to kill time before the final whistle blew."

The crowd was around the playing field by then, the Yale people ready to assault the goal posts. But not Halsey. He climbed down from the press box on the shaky ladder and headed home, writing later, "I dropped away from the stadium as limp as the lettuce in a table d'hôte salad."

13

How Could We Have Lost to *That* Team!

The players had more difficulty than Professor Halsey in getting off the field and leaving the stadium because of the milling, mischievous throng. One group…seemingly Yales…attacked the steel goal posts, embedded in concrete, and it took a long time to bend and break the metal tubes.

Stan Fuller had his helmet off, "Carrying it like I always did. The equipment people would come and take it and pack it. So I let go when somebody grabbed it.

"The next week I got a letter from some youngster thanking me. He said he was captain of his team and the only one with a helmet. I never got it back."

Kelley was disoriented. "Physically, emotionally and mentally exhausted," he said. "Two guys were holding me up as we were trying to find the way to the field house."

Merri Scott, the tackle, said, "I'm not one who cries at football games. But I started sobbing and I grabbed a guy and asked how to get out of here and he took me through the tunnel (at the north end of the stadium) and to the field house. There people were pushing and pounding on me, lots of people, old Yale heroes like Ted Coy and Tad Jones.

"That's the first I heard that only eleven of us had played the entire game. We'd been too busy to give it a thought."

Who had the football, the treasured prize of victory? DeAngelis, the Yale center, had it and was not giving it up. Someone had already snatched his helmet. He dodged and darted his way but once out of the stadium slowed to a walk on the path to the field house. "By then they just wanted to pat me on the back," he said.

The Princeton athletes did not fare so well. "You can't imagine the furor that was created by our losing this game," said Gil Lea. "The feelings were very intense against us, among alumni, friends, everyone. They swarmed around the field house, just furious with us."

Lea many times in later years claimed that some in the horde even spat on the players.

There was a gentle mob within the Yale dressing room. "Everyone who'd ever played for Yale seemed to be there," said Roscoe, who did not remember taking a shower, dressing or walking down to the waiting train in the yards. His cheek was sore, swollen and throbbing, from the blow by a Princeton helmet on his sixth punt return.

Two former Yale players now junior varsity assistant coaches, Walter Levering and Century Milstead, were not in the locker room but up at Harvard Stadium scouting the Crimson in its 47-3 victory over New Hampshire. When the score was announced…Princeton 0, Yale 7…Levering, a recent 5-foot-9, 160-pound halfback, turned to Milstead, a robust 6-2, 220, former tackle who had played for the New York Giants, and lifted Century right off his seat. "I never could have done that again," he told me 70 years later.

Lew Wallace and son Billy left Palmer's unsympathetic cement seats on the visiting team's east side of the stadium and went to a dormitory to visit with Billy's first cousin, Robert Failey, from Indianapolis. He was a Princeton freshman and didn't have much to say. We then headed for home, four hours away in the dark, frazzled but contented.

Coach Crisler had the good sense to protect his players and he did not want them abroad that evening, exposed on Prospect Street where the undergraduate social clubs lay. So after they'd dressed he had them pile into buses and away they went, five miles back to The Lawrenceville School where they had spent the previous evening in a large dormitory attic.

"We didn't even see our families that night," said Lea. "We sat up 'til one, two o'clock in the morning with blankets around our shoulders bemoaning the game.

"How could we have lost to *That* team? We had so much talent.

"And to be beaten by just eleven men. That was the first time this really sank in for us. We vowed that next year every time we saw a Yalie standing up we were going to knock him down. And we did."

Princeton won, 38-7, in 1935 at the Yale Bowl. But it wasn't enough. There would never be enough reprisal.

Arrangements had been made in advance for the Yale team en route home to stay overnight at the Hotel New Yorker across the street from the Pennsylvania Station. They would go to the theater to see a hit musical comedy, *Life Begins at 8:40*, starring Ray Bolger and Bert Lahr with the score by Harold Arlen and Ira Gershwin.

"It was prearranged," Roscoe suspected, "with the thought we would need something to cheer us up after taking a beating. Anyway, it was a very nice gesture and much appreciated by those who saw the show, who were introduced as the show began and received a loud, long and very enthusiastic welcome."

Or so Jerry was told. He was in a hotel bed, in pain. DeAngelis says he went but he slept through the show.

Pat Garvan, the manager, had a bottle of champagne delivered to the room of each of the eleven newly minted Ironmen, another very nice gesture.

Roscoe added, "I tried to eat some supper with little success, and went right up to bed, as did several others. And then began the longest night of my life. I was so jazzed up replaying the game, exhausted and still dehydrated (which I didn't realize fully) and with my face pounding, I couldn't get to sleep. I remember looking at my watch at 3:30 AM and I still hadn't slept. Wake up call at 8 AM, breakfast, bus to Grand Central, train to New Haven and into my own bed as fast as I could get there. Bliss."

The Sunday newspapers were full of the game, of course. Stanley Woodward began his account in the *Herald Tribune* as follows: "Eleven Yale football players with constitutions of iron and dispositions of wild cats perpetrated the signal outrage of modern athletics in Princeton's Palmer Stadium today."

Robert Kelley in the *Times* was no less animated: "Yale defeated Princeton today by a score of 7-0. In that sentence is packed all the deep excitement of the most popular drama that football or any other sport knows, the rise of the man without a chance, the refusal of the underdog to play the role that has been assigned to him."

Both Kelley and Woodward explained how thoroughly Yale had outplayed Princeton. So did Roscoe later on. He wrote, "Princeton outgained us on the ground 185 yards to 71. But 133 of those yards came in two bursts, two drives. The first towards the end of the 2nd period, the second in the 3rd period when they went 63 yds. in 10 plays, all on the ground.

"That means for the balance of the game Princeton's offense gained only nine yards in seven carries on the ground and zero yards in four pass attempts, none completed, two intercepted. Those figures, plus that we held on both goal-line stands, attests to the game being won by the Yale defense."

Stanley Woodward had a confirmation in Monday's *Herald Tribune*. "Yale's defensive alignment was a 6-2-2-1. Three linemen, Clare Curtin, Jack Wright and Ben Grosscup, shifted positions on offense and defense. Curtin was right defensive tackle and left offensive guard; Wright was right offensive tackle and right defensive guard; Grosscup was right offensive guard and left defensive guard. Both guards and tackles played great defensive football, flying across the line when the ball moved."

Woodward, the old Amherst tackle, added, "In my opinion Wright stood out a little above the others. His defensive charge was such an atrocity that he frequently carried two Tiger linemen into the backfield with him. Wright murdered the left side of the Princeton line."

There were other accolades for Kelley and Train, the ends, and DeAngelis and Whitehead, the linebackers.

Because the *Sun* published no edition on Sunday the poet laureate of Yale football, George Trevor, waited a day and then his copy in the Monday evening paper spilled over four columns. Trevor set eight scenes in chronological order surrounding the game…several of his own imagination but glorious copy…and ended with a stanza from a Yale hymn.

Mother of men grown strong in giving
Honor to them thy light hath led;
Rich in the toil of thousands living,

Brave in the deeds of thousands dead.
Thee whom our fathers loved before us,
Thee whom our sons unborn shall hail.
Praise we today in sturdy chorus
*Mother of men—Old Yale.**

Contemporary Yale had another game to play, against Harvard in the Yale Bowl the next Saturday. Roscoe, who had lost 11 pounds in part due to trainer Wandle's no-water dictum, didn't get back to 160 until Wednesday. The same was true for Curtin who had gone from 225 down to 209. Practice that week amounted to scouting reports and mostly walk-throughs, meaning walking through offensive plays and defensive schemes planned for Harvard. There were no injuries although Whitehead limped a lot.

Fortunately the Crimson had a weak team that autumn, having won just three games, and Yale was somewhat somnambulant in winning a dull contest, 14-0, before a crowd of 55,000…18,000 short of the Bowl's capacity but remarkable nevertheless.

The second of the two touchdowns came on a 15-yard pass play, Roscoe to Kelley. It was the first time since 1923 that a Yale team…a Big Three champion having beaten both Harvard and Princeton…had held both rivals scoreless.

The Harvard captain and right guard, Herman (Gunny) Gundlach, thus concluded four seasons of playing opposite DeAngelis nose to nose and five across from Curtin, whom he had first encountered in 1930 when his unbeaten Worcester Academy team lost to Exeter, 3-0, on Curtin's field goal.

---

* The complete story can be found in the Appendix.

Yale coaching staff, 1935. L. to R. Gerald Ford (future President of the U.S.), Stewart Scott, Trainer Frank Wandle, Dennis Myers, Raymond Pond, Earle Neale, Ivan Williamson, Walter Levering.

My father had a bunch of Harvard tickets for my mother and out-of-town guests but not one for me, flushed with Yale enthusiasm. So I sulked, even whined to no avail, and was left at home.

The previous Saturday had been a big one for college football relative to attendance, supporting Roscoe's contention that the games took people out of their depressions over the Depression. Fourteen contests, reported the New York *Times,* drew 510,000 spectators, leading with Michigan at Ohio State, 68,000. Princeton's crowd for Yale, 53,000, had been the second largest.

Conspicuously absent on Monday morning was the *Daily Princetonian*, the university's newspaper. It simply was not published. And without any explanation then or the following day when the football news was the team's beginning preparation for the season's finale against Dartmouth.* Perhaps the editors had decided to forget about the Yale game...pretend it never happened.

The Monday after the season's end brought the election of the Yale captain for the next season and then the annual football banquet at The Fence Club, the former Psi Upsilon fraternity house off York Street. Twenty-four players were eligible to vote because they had been in a game against Harvard, if only briefly, in 1933 or 1934. The junior candidates from the Class of 1936 were Roscoe, Train and Whitehead. The decision was Whitehead and the vote announced as unanimous by custom, although it probably was not on the first ballot.

Three dozen telegrams and almost as many letters of congratulations poured forth to Whitehead. One of the most interesting was from Winthrop H. Brooks, president of Brooks Brothers in New York, in which he brought up "the matter of representing us" in New Haven.

What was this...commerce rearing in an age of innocence? A subtle endorsement by the Yale captain in exchange for haberdashery perhaps? Oh, woe.

Whitehead backed off after a talk with Malcolm Farmer, the athletic director. Mr. Brooks understood. "Possible criticism might arise," he wrote. "I note that you say you will be glad to take up the work after the closing of the *(next)* football season, and I would be most pleased to have you do so then."

Mr. Brooks was also interested in Roscoe. "If Mr. Roscoe has planned to come to New York, it would be a very good

---

* The Tigers crushed the Indians, 38-13.

plan for him to drop in and see me at the store." Roscoe never mentioned the incident, the occasion. Under the present rules of the National Collegiate Athletic Association, each would have been declared ineligible for having taken even one sock from Brooks.

The football season had ended and Alabama…not Princeton…was chosen to go to the Rose Bowl representing the East. The Crimson Tide defeated Stanford, 29-13, on New Year's day, 1935, thanks to a passing pair of Dixie Howell and Don Hutson. But undefeated Minnesota had been accorded the national championship by acclaim.

Basketball practice had already begun. DeAngelis, a returning starter, and Kelley, a promising sophomore, joined the varsity.

An Associated Press poll of national sportswriters declared the Yale victory over Princeton to be sport's *upset of the year.* Campus life moved on.

The undergraduates' favorite movie was *It Happened One Night,* starring steamy Clark Gable and the pert Claudette Colbert. It won an Academy award as best picture of the year, and the sale of undershirts fell off dramatically, it was claimed, because Gable in the film had bared his chest, exposing nakedness above the waist.

The committee for the Yale Junior Promenade, the social highlight of the winter season, met for the first time to help plan the event scheduled for March 8, 1935. The football squad was well represented. John Hersey was chairman, Kim Whitehead floor manager, Webb Davis the treasurer, Tommy Curtin, Bernie Rankin and Jerry Roscoe members.

Junior Prom leaders, Davis, Hersey, Whitehead.

Hersey, the writer and educator who became probably the most celebrated member of a Yale class, 1936, replete with notables, had been a reserve end behind Bob Train. But Train was so good, so valuable, that he seldom came off the field. "John was a tremendous left-footed punter," said Roscoe. "Because of the substitution rules he never had a chance to get in a game and kick."

Hersey, whose first novel, *A Bell for Adano,* would gain him a Pulitzer prize in 1945, was not the complaining type.

Feisty Webb Davis, the captain of their freshman team as a 5-foot-7, 160-pound guard, was wistful rather than complaining. He told friends he would have given "anything" to have played in the Princeton game, to have been an Ironman.

Bernie Rankin

Tommy Curtin, no relation to Clare Curtin, was a talented tailback-quarterback who had replaced Roscoe in the Army game when the latter was ill with grippe. Tommy died the next year, a month before graduation, of a blood disease, leucopenia. "My best friend on the team," mourned Jerry Roscoe.

Rankin, a regular displaced by Fuller and thus not an Ironman by coaching decision, was handsome enough to go to Hollywood. But he became a lawyer instead.*

* A classmate, Bowen Charleton Tufts, did go to Hollywood and became actor Sonny Tufts. An autographed photograph of Sonny hung in the barroom of the DKE fraternity house for a few decades.

14

Stover & Whitehead, Merriwell & Coy

Kim and Betty

In the sport's adolescence the boys who were good at football chose their colleges through a variety of coincidental circumstances...some transparent, some shady. There was no such device as the athletic scholarship although financial help could be made available in a variety of ways, some clear, some dusky. A bird dog...the familiar term for seekers of talent...could be a secondary school coach, an old grad, a sportswriter, almost anybody.

The best recruiter Yale probably ever had in the 20th century's early years was a novelist. That would have been Owen Johnson, Class of 1901, who wrote *Stover at Yale*, published in 1911.

Supposedly a satire on collegiate conformity and snobbery, it had enormous popularity. However many an impressionable youth saw Dink Stover...magnificent athlete, able student, admired class figure...only as someone to emulate. And Yale, Eli Yale, was the place to go if one could get there.

There were facets of Stover, and also Frank Merriwell,* to be found in the person of Mather Kimball Whitehead, the Ironmen's fullback. Kim was a sturdy 5 feet 11, 180 pounds, ruggedly handsome, an honor student, the modest, quiet recipient of the rewards and awards that came to a Yale football captain.

He was born in Buffalo, the home city of his parents, James and Anne Kimball Whitehead. The father, a Cornell graduate, moved the family to Westfield, N.J., an attractive suburban village 25 miles west of New York City, when the son was three months old.

---

* A figurative literary cousin of Stover, Merriwell was the fictional hero of more than 100 of Gilbert Patten's dime novels (they cost 10 cents) published between 1896 and 1916. Merriwell also was a Yale man.

Kim showed prowess as an athlete at Pingry, a private day school in nearby Elizabeth, and was captain of the football team in his senior year. Then it was decided the 17-year-old Whitehead should take an extra year before college at Andover, the mighty Massachusetts prep school that sent graduates in droves to Yale.

There were six, the most from any secondary school, on Yale's 1934 squad of 28, and Whitehead was the only regular. He had been a standout from the first day Yale coaches laid eyes on him as a freshman; a varsity regular beginning with the first game of his sophomore season in 1933 as either a halfback or a fullback, sometimes a punter, and always a ferocious linebacker. Among his teammates his nickname was Happy, a jest because he was so dour, so mean as a football player. He hit hard and gave no quarter. No wonder the coaches adored him, as much as did the women.

Captain Mather Kimball Whitehead

His appeal was universal. Mrs. James Rowland Angell, the wife of the Yale's president, wrote him a note of congratulations upon his captaincy as did Agnes Farmer, spouse of the athletic director, Malcolm Farmer. They would be hostesses at the teas, the social functions Yale proposed to hold following football games in the upstairs lounge of the Ray Tompkins House, the athletic administrative headquarters in downtown New Haven a mile and a half from the Bowl. An appearance by the football captain was anticipated.*

The Whiteheads were comfortable but not wealthy. There was an older brother, who had graduated from Yale in 1932, and a sister. Kim qualified every year for a significant scholarship given by the Yale Club of New York City, which always favored athletes with its benevolences.

In his junior and senior years he held one of the most sought-after employments the university offered...the cushy task of being an aide to the master of a residential college. For Whitehead it was Berkeley College and Charles Seymour, distinguished professor of history and next (1937) President of Yale. The appointment gave the recipient free room and board.

Then there were the summer jobs. A good one came in 1934. Whitehead would be a tutor-companion at a small summer colony, Nonquitt, Mass., for the family of John B. Hollister, a partner in the significant Cincinnati law firm of Taft, Stettinius & Hollister. John Hollister, Yale Class of 1913, held the local "Republican Taft" seat in the Congress at the time while a senior partner, Robert A. Taft, Yale Class of

---

* "Polite and gracious but deadly and obligatory," recalled Bill Stack, the 1939 captain, in 1995.

1910, planned his successful campaign for election to the U.S. Senate in 1938.

Whitehead did well with his charges, Jack, age 9; Alice, 13, and Anne, 16. At summer's end Ellen Hollister felt compelled, as one mother to another, to write: "My dear Mrs. Whitehead. I must write you a few words to tell you how we have all enjoyed Kim this summer. He couldn't have been more perfect and he fitted into our household so easily.

"Being a tutor is a very difficult job, I think, for you necessarily become a member of the family, and I have seen some rather trying instances of that right here in Nonquitt.

"Kim was always so considerate…constantly finding things to do to be helpful, and I shall miss him very much. I really think you would be proud of him. I hope some day we may meet you."

Congressman Hollister was plenty proud of his tutor. Following the grand season and the election he wrote Whitehead, on Cincinnati law-firm stationary but with a Congressional envelope bearing his own three-cent stamp, a warm personal letter in pen and ink on November 27, 1934.

"I have known a number of Yale football captains in my time and I know of none who better deserve, by nature of character, leadership and true playing ability, the election you have received."

The Yale captain-elect was in demand. Society seemed to be shaking off the dinginess of the depression and invitations to debutante parties in New York, Boston and elsewhere came to Yale Station. Whitehead, who attended a few, passed on to his mother the formal cards of invitation which she saved along with sports-page clippings from the New York,

New Haven and Newark newspapers. Everything went into two large brown scrapbooks.*

Edgar Church welcomed Captain Whitehead in 1935 to Philadelphia's Franklin Field where Yale had not played since 1889 when Church was Penn's captain.

One invitation Whitehead seized was an expense-paid trip to Chicago right after Christmas to speak at a Yale Club father-and-son luncheon there. He then went up to Milwaukee, where the family had relatives.

We are uncertain if on that visit he did, or did not yet, meet Elisabeth Ilma Uihlein, the Schlitz brewing heiress whom he would marry and who, some claimed, shackled his later life.

---

* Whitehead in turn saved the scrapbooks and, following his death, June 12, 1995, Bill Wallace rescued them from being thrown out during a clearing of the Whitehead residence in Fairfield, Conn.

Or at the least exposed the hero's Achilles heel, the indolence associated with alcohol.

When the Junior Promenade in Woolsey Hall came around on March 8, 1935, floor manager Whitehead was listed in the program as "stag," meaning he had no date. "Unaccompanied," said the New York *Herald Tribune*.

But his mother, Mrs. James H. Whitehead, came up from Westfield to be one of the 22 promenade patronesses that John Hersey's committee needed to provide. These women, who included Mrs. Angell and other prominent Yale spouses, were chaperones on hand to help the 1,500 girl guests solve whatever problems might arise during the gala weekend.

Jim DeAngelis, who had neither tuxedo nor tolerance for the Yale social life, did not participate. He was too busy playing basketball, hitting the books, aiming toward graduation, and worrying about what kind of a job he might be able to get. The Blakeslee dole had to end sometime.

When the football season came around the next fall DeAngelis did have a job, at Yale as an assistant for Reg Root, the head freshman coach. Clare Curtin, in graduate school, and DeAngelis coached the linemen, each being paid $2,500.

The varsity coaches needed to find replacements for those two and four other Ironmen. Fuller, Grosscup and Morton had graduated and Scott had left college for a year. There were plenty of backs among the newcomers, the sophomores, but not the needed linemen.

The leading backs were Charley Ewart, a 5-foot-7 quarterback who took playing time away from Roscoe; tailback Clint Frank, who would become one of Yale's most celebrated players ever and the 1937 Heisman Trophy winner, and Al Hessberg, the elusive new wingback with sprinter speed.

Whitehead, recovered from an appendicitis operation, remained at fullback. Denny Myers cobbled together a lightweight line and the team won six of nine games. The losses were to Army; to Dartmouth for the first time in history, and to Princeton at the Bowl in the season's final game.

The Tigers, with Pepper Constable their captain, won in a rout, 38-7, completing an undefeated campaign in which they outscored nine opponents, 256 to 32. Yale's touchdown was scored by Kelley on a pass from Roscoe, completing a 29-yard play late in the mismatch.

Constable and Whitehead met at midfield for the tossing of the coin to determine who would gain the choice of kicking off or receiving. It was the last of four games among the athletes of the classes of 1936…"a hell of a rivalry," Jerry Roscoe would call it.

At the demise of the respective captains half a century later Constable was adored and revered by his college and community, Whitehead a lonely alcoholic whose last recorded communication with Old Eli was a letter to the athletic director grousing about the parking problem he'd had at a Harvard-Yale game.

The following June brought graduation for 1936, "Yale's greatest class" as it was often described on account of its many luminaries, some by way of inheritance and more through achievement such as this dozen: Bill Beinecke, Robert Berliner, Jonathan Bingham, Lloyd Cutler, David Dellinger, Peter Grace, August Heckscher, John Hersey, Dick Pinkham, Dillon Ripley, Dick Rossbach and Walt Rostow.

Kim Whitehead would not be on any such compilation. He graduated with honors; had been elected to Skull & Bones, the distinguished senior secret society,* and listed his next intention as attending law school.

40th Reunion, 1974, posed under the Walter Camp Memorial Arch outside Yale Bowl. Front: Kelley, Wright, Grosscup, DeAngelis, Curtin, Scott, Train. Rear; Whitehead, Roscoe, Fuller. Ten of 11.

But he went to Wall Street instead, as a corporate bond underwriter and salesman. On June 28, 1939, he married Betty Uihlein of the family that, along with the Pabst clan,

* The football captain, as well as the chairman of the Yale *Daily News,* were usually automatic Skull & Bones electees. So among the Ironmen the three team captains, Curtin, Whitehead and Kelley, were members as well as two others, Stan Fuller and Choo Choo Train, for no particular reason anyone cold fathom other than football celebrity.

made Milwaukee famous as a brewery town. Jerry Roscoe was an usher in the wedding.

The couple lived in Plainfield, N.J., and Kim commuted to New York until August, 1942, when he entered the Navy as a commissioned officer in the administrative branch of Naval Aviation. He served at airfields in Charlestown, R.I., and Groton, Conn., where carrier air groups were trained, and finally at Floyd Bennett Field in Brooklyn. He was discharged with the rank of lieutenant commander late in 1945.

Soon thereafter Kim and Betty moved to Fairfield and commenced remodeling a large old house on Burr Street, abutting the Merritt Parkway. A featured attraction of this residence was a handsomely landscaped swimming pool with an attached party barn. There were plenty of parties as the vivacious Mrs. Whitehead, who happened to be a superb gardener, lived to entertain.

Whitehead embarked on a series of intangible jobs with outfits like Independent Economic Research Foundation, Bristol Bearings Corporation, and International Mining Corporation. In a report for the 30-year class book, in 1966, he described his interests as horseback riding, tennis, golf and gardening. He wrote, "I made one trip around the world by air and would like to travel more."

They had no children, which was too bad, said friends in later years. One said, "Whenever Kim talked about 'doing something,' like getting a real job, Betty would put him off. She'd say something like, 'You don't need to do that. We've got plenty of money.' She wouldn't let him go."

50th Reunion, 1984. L. to R. Kelley, Grosscup, DeAngelis, Curtin, Whitehead, Scott, Train. Seven of 11. Bill Lutz, foreground, represented his absent grandfather, Roscoe.

There was a lot of drinking…around the pool in summer, within the big comfortable house in winter. Jack Field, a Yale contemporary who had been a jayvee football player, lived nearby with his wife, Priscilla, and they were occasional guests.

"It was pretty hard to keep up," Field told me many years later. He described an evening when he and his wife left a party at Burr Street, went home and to bed. They were awakened hours later by the sound of gravel being thrown against their bedroom window.

Betty and Kim were standing in their driveway urging the Fields to "come on down" and have a nightcap. "I guess we did," said Field. "Kim's life was tragic," he added. "He had everything, brains, connections. All for nothing."

Bertrand Russell, in *The Conquest of Happiness*, wrote, "Drunkenness is temporary suicide; the happiness that it brings is merely negative, a momentary cessation of unhappiness."

That might have applied to the Whiteheads. Health issues arose, first with Betty who died in 1984. Kim had diabetic problems which led to an amputation of his right leg. He lived out his final years in a wheelchair, attended by devoted servants, and he was not much fun, grumpy and complaining.

When the class of 1936 published *Fifty Years Out* in 1986, Whitehead merely wrote for his biography, "Widowed" and "Retired." He was ill, alone, and had given up most of life. Nine years later he was dead, at 81, and the brief obituaries mentioned the Ironmen only in passing.

60th Reunion, 1994. Kelley, DeAngelis, Scott, Roscoe, Whitehead in front. Five of 11.

In terms of a Yale hero finding life after football to be hard, Whitehead would qualify, if not as dramatically as an earlier one. That would be Ted Coy, who died in September, 1935, 27 days before Whitehead's final season in the Bowl began.

Coy, the son of the first headmaster of The Hotchkiss School, entered Yale in 1906. He was named an all-American all three varsity seasons in which Yale lost only once, and he served as captain of the 1909 team...unbeaten, untied and unscored upon.

Captain Edward Harris Coy.

In writing a tribute, *One For Valhalla,* for a Yale football program, George Trevor described the high-stepping fullback who ran over opponents as "trim of line, broad of shoulder with the leonine mop of curly yellow hair. He seemed to personify life, dynamic motion, irresistible force. They have buried his body but his spirit lives on, woven into the very fabric of Yale football."

Coy worked for a coal company in Chattanooga, Tenn., for a bank in Washington, D.C., as a broker on Wall Street, and lastly as a salesman for an insurance firm whose head was an old Yale football man, Foster Sanford.

Coy's first wife obtained a divorce in Paris in 1925 and the former football ace created something of a tabloid sensation when he soon after married Jeanne Eagles, the actress and star of the racy Broadway play "Rain." They divorced three years later and Coy married again.

He declared bankruptcy in 1933, listing assets of $750 against debt of $13,672, and saying, "I've carried my burden for so long I've got to let it down to regain a little strength."

He died at the age of 47 in New York of pneumonia while living with his sister in an apartment on East 54th Street. The obituary in the New York Times ran to two full columns.

15

Jerry Roscoe & Pepper Constable

World War II marked every American. Those wars that came after...Korea, Vietnam, Gulf and Iraq...were pipsqueak as to scale. During WWII the armed forces numbered 15 million men and women, with uncounted millions more participating in the war effort, as it was popularly called, that went into all corners of the country.

The ages of the Ironmen, when caught up in the immensity, were 26 to 32. Strat Morton went first, in 1940, and he was the one who did not come back, killed on a training flight in Georgia in June, 1941. At that time Kim Whitehead was in New York helping a classmate, Richard (Red) Moore, direct a public interest outfit called College Men for Defense, one dedicated to keeping the United States out of the "European" war. "What did we know?" said Whitehead afterward.

The call to service went these ways.

Clare Curtin, who had become a prep school English teacher and adjacent football coach, received a master's degree at Columbia in 1943 before going into the Navy for three years. He never told what he did or where, except he was a senior-grade lieutenant at discharge.

DeAngelis stayed at Yale as an assistant coach until 1940, the year the new athletic director, Ogden (Oggie) Miller, made it clear to Pond and his staff that their contracts would not be renewed after three consecutive losing seasons, the last a dismal 1-7.

Pond became head coach at Bates College in Lewiston, Maine, and loyal DeAngelis followed. Soon Jim was in the Navy as a lieutenant directing physical training for aviation cadets and next as a flight-deck officer on a small aircraft carrier named the USS. Lunga Point that never got in harm's way.

Stan Fuller first joined Goodrich Tire & Rubber in Akron, Ohio, and then switched to Goodyear Aircraft in the same city which by 1941 had a number of defense contracts. These made him, a personnel executive, exempt from military service during the war years.

After college Ben Grosscup, whose nickname was 'Gross,' fooled around with sales jobs in New York, Pittsburgh and St. Louis. Then came the Navy and a hot war for him in the Pacific where he earned a medal, a Bronze Star. As a squadron officer he helped to keep the planes flying off the decks of the carriers Lexington and Saratoga, and off the deck at Guadalcanal too in the anxious autumn of 1942.

When combat had calmed down, a Yale friend was not surprised to find Lt. (j.g.) Grosscup in charge of the officers' club on the island of Ulithi, the Navy's supply and rest-and-recreation base for the South Pacific. Ben was the go-to guy for a case of Scotch.

Kelley, like Fuller, was never in any service. He failed Navy physical minimums on account of ear problems and held jobs in defense companies. My final chapter confronts this touchy issue.

Roscoe joined Pan American Airways, founded and run by men of Yale, a year after college and his career with this vital organization carried into and through the war. He held a Navy commission and sometimes wore a uniform while setting up bases in many places.

Meredith Scott, who did not graduate from Yale, was a high school football coach, a real estate broker, a shipyard worker and a cargo checker back in coastal Virginia before joining in the Navy in 1940. He spent 42 months at sea, mostly on destroyers, and made that service a career, retiring in 1962 as a satisfied lieutenant commander.

Robert Train spent four years in the Navy, 1941–1945, and like so many WWII servicemen he made little of the time, the experience, in subsequent commentary. Train in his tour went from able seaman, the lowest grade, on up to Lieutenant Commander. His contributions came aboard vessels chasing and destroying Nazi submarines off the Atlantic Coast.

Jack Wright had two more seasons of fun and football following the Ironmen's year as did his roommate, Larry Kelley. After graduation in 1937 Wright joined a training program run by R.H. Macy, the New York department store, having no other smart ideas. Two years later he became a distributor for Chevrolet, also in New York, and he joined the Navy in August, 1942, as a lieutenant junior grade. He was first assigned to Panama, and then came the Pacific campaigns of 1944 and 1945, the Marshall Islands, the Gilberts, Saipan, Palau. He too was discharged as a lieutenant commander.

So eight of the Ironmen were Naval officers. When the war ended, so did the similarities. The 10 survivors went their ways.

Curtin wound teaching English at Needham High School outside Boston for more than 40 years. His football past had no meaning to him and he turned me down on the telephone when I asked for an interview in 2002, politely saying, "I forgot all about it long ago."

I tried again in 2004, when he was 93, and the Ironmen's captain said, "That's history. I don't think about it. We came off the field, we'd won the game and Ducky Pond said, 'You're iron men.' But don't quote me on that."*

DeAngelis was back at New Haven and Yale in 1946 as head coach of the freshman team. Howard Odell had taken over as the varsity head coach in 1942 and had produced an undefeated team in 1944. Then Odell left for the University of Washington after 1947, taking his staff with him, including Reggie Root.

DeAngelis detoured to the University of Toledo for a season and for another at the University of Nebraska before rejoining Odell and friends at Seattle in 1950. When Odell and his staff were fired in 1952 DeAngelis, at the insistence of his wife, gave up coaching and returned to New Haven. He sold automobiles, Buicks, for five years and then became the best concrete pipe salesman in southern New England for the Leonard company in Hamden, a job that took him to his retirement in 1991.

Along the way the plucky little center helped organize and host the Ironmen's three reunions in New Haven, and he seldom missed a home game in the Bowl.

Fuller went home to Erie and had a long association as personnel director with two companies, Tosco Plastics and Fenestra Inc. He also pursued an interest in the criminal justice system, first as a probation officer and then as a juvenile

---

* Just as well, as Pond didn't tell them anything as far as anyone else could recall.

court administrator in Toledo, Oh., where he had relocated. He was 96 when he died in 1998.

Grosscup wound up in Pittsburgh, where he started and ran a soft drink company and after that a seed company. He was a major figure in the Harvard-Yale-Princeton Club of Pittsburgh and a jolly good fellow. He died in 1993.

Scott, after his Navy retirement, became a Virginia farmer not far from Charlottesville and also had an insurance business in Culpeper, Va. He died in 2004.

Bob Train attained the presidency in 1956 of a cotton company, Bibb Manufacturing, in Macon, Ga., that he had joined in 1937. "Am an arch conservative," he wrote for the 25th Reunion book, and believed Yale had gone down because of "a de-emphasis on athletics" and "too much emphasis on scholastic standing." At the time of the 50th Reunion he had retired and mellowed. His interests were, he wrote, "Golf, fishing and booze." He died in 1988.

The easy-gong Jack Wright became a management consultant, working for McKinsey and W.R. Grace in New York, and then as an executive recruiter. He lived in Chappaqua in Westchester County and he told his classmates, in a reunion biography, "I'm plodding along in a fat, dumb and more or less happy but undistinguished manner." He retired in 1973 and died five years later.

Roscoe's life had distinction in it. As a youth he was disarming and charming but also disciplined, possibly due to a military background. His father had been Regular Army, a polo-playing Cavalry officer who had served with Douglas MacArthur in the Philippines at the turn of the century, and Jerry was born at Fort Leavenworth in Kansas. The father was retired and the family living in San Diego by the time Roscoe was sent east to prep school, his beloved Kent in the

Litchfield Hills of Connecticut, a four-day train trip from home.

Jerome Verity Roscoe

Greasy Neale was the perfect mentor for the dutiful Roscoe and the two bloomed when it came to shaping the Yale offense…what plays to call in which situations. Because the rules dictated that coaches could have no part in selecting plays, the game's destiny lay with the quarterback, and the crafty Neale would have Roscoe be his second self.

The bonding began that first summer of their relationship, 1934, through the correspondence between the Boyer Ranch in Savery, Wyo., where Roscoe had a job as a ranch hand, and Lost Creek, W.Va. From there Neale wrote, on stationary from The Waldo, a 'fire-proof hotel' in nearby Clarksburg, that Roscoe's answers to the coach's questions…what play to call in varying situations…were "practically perfect."

Neale was careful with his compliments, because he did not wish his charge "to get the big head." Still the coach could be effusive. "You are the best Q.B. pupil I have ever had. In a very short time you learned the system better than any one I have ever known."

Roscoe kept the letter. Wouldn't you?

The next summer Neale wrote, "I want you to be perfect in 1935. However, I will say you are the best in America, but you can do better. A great quarter back in 1934 does not make you a wonder in 1935. Study your attack."

Roscoe sustained his friendship with his coach for four decades. During those years Jerry became a man in a grey-flannel suit, the consummate New York advertising executive with a home in the suburbs, Rye, New York; a wife, Patricia; three daughters, Nancy, Cynthia and Alison; and a good golf game.

Roscoe had performed a variety of tasks for Pan American Airways for 14 years, the most important of which was establishing bases in Alaska during World War II. Pan Am had a contract with the Air Transport Command to supply the Army outposts in the Aleutian Islands, and Roscoe was the assistant manager.

Ad Man. This sketch from the J. Walter Thompson in-house publication.

In 1951, weary of travel and with a growing family, Roscoe joined the premier New York advertising agency of J. Walter Thompson as the Pan Am account executive.

Then Chester J. LaRoche, an old Yale quarterback and a founder of the National Football Foundation and College Hall of Fame, persuaded Roscoe to join his smaller advertising agency as a senior vice-president, a position Jerry held until his retirement at the end of 1975.

Roscoe, who had been much involved with the elite United States Senior Golf Association, eagerly moved to Pinehurst, N.C., where he could play almost every day.

He had always been a faithful alumnus, never missing a class reunion, serving on the university's athletic board of control and as a member of a panel formed to select a new football coach in 1963.*

At Pinehurst, Jerry had come across Sumner Rulon-Miller Jr., more generally known as Ippy, who had been a reserve running back on the Princeton teams of 1933–1935. They played golf two or three times a week for 12 years. On a course one day, said Roscoe, "Ippy had stroke while I was talking to him and dropped unconscious. He died a week later."

From Pinehurst, Roscoe later moved to a retirement community, Lake Ridge, in Virginia and died there on Christmas Day, 2003. He was 91.

In 1986, the night before the Yale game at Princeton, the Tiger players of the Class of 1936 held a reunion there to celebrate a 50th anniversary and their four grand seasons in which they had won every game but one.

The Ironmen, who had induced that defeat, were graciously invited but the only one who could attend was Roscoe, the perfect, popular emissary. He recalled, "We swapped stories and feelings without rancor…their three wins and our one…but with mutual fun and admiration.

"They were fiercely and deservedly proud of their accomplishments. Yet that one game stuck in their craws so badly it seemingly outweighed all their other wins combined."

---

* The choice was John Pont, who stayed for only two seasons and was succeeded by his assistant, Carmen Cozza, head coach for 32 years, 1965–1996.

Captain William Pepper Constable

That evening Roscoe renewed his friendship with Gil Lea, the Princeton end who had also been in advertising…"the rat race" in New York. Lea, who later became a directory publisher in Maine and then retired to Vero Beach, Fla., had often claimed that he had almost gotten to Roscoe as Jerry let go the fateful touchdown pass to Kelley. Another couple of inches, another couple of seconds.

Roscoe, however, responded that he was oblivious to Lea's presence, his threat. Stalemate.

The catalyst of this Princeton group was Pepper Constable, their senior captain and fullback to whom they always looked for comfort, consistency. Constable, however, had written a dark sentence in the 50th anniversary class book earlier that year. "Have been fighting Alzheimer's." That chilled Lea who called Constable "my best friend," as did other teammates.

Constable was from a Princeton clan in Baltimore and Pepper the middle name from a family connection more befitting than William as in W. Pepper Constable. It was a likely nomen, verb or noun, for this athlete and big-man-on-campus…class president every year.

Constable became a doctor and for many years was chief of medicine at the Princeton Medical Center. He had chosen to live in his college town and he married in 1951 a Yale girl…Betty Howe, from New Haven, whose father and brother were accomplished Yale athletes.

Pepper Constable in 1981.

Betty Constable was an athlete too, a squash player who won the women's national championship five times and was seldom beaten. She coached Princeton women's squash for 20 years, and her teams captured one national championship after another.

Reunions in June have always been a major feature on the Princeton calendar and when they came around the informal headquarters for the Class of 1936 was at the Constable backyard. There Pepper's players draped themselves in their tartan orange and black reunion jackets, drank beer and smoked cigars.

In the winter of 1981 Betty was shocked when Pepper said to her, "When the day comes and I have lost my brain, I hope I'll have enough sense to end my life."

She was unaware of the Alzheimer's disease, but he was not. "As the caretaker of my husband, I had a dark cloud always hanging over me," she wrote in an article for the *Princeton Alumni Weekly* after his death in 1986.*

"It was hard for me to have the patience to bend with his mood changes and his frustrations. He became a man I didn't know. At one point he said to me, 'Betty, please remember, I am not the same man you married.'"

They struggled along until the summer of 1986, when they had a house in Nantucket on Hulbert, the waterfront street running along the shore overlooking Nantucket Sound.

"One night Pepper went to bed earlier than I. When I went upstairs I found him sitting on the edge of his bed. When I asked him what was the matter, he said, 'I can't sleep.' Those were his last words to me.

"The next morning he was gone. His pajamas lay by the door that led to the ocean. That was his message. He had sacrificed himself for all of us, knowing all too well the suffering we would have had to bear had he lived on."

Constable was aware, and had said so, that swallowing a lot of water was an effective way to take one's life. His body, 73 years old, was found two days later off Great Point at the northeast tip of Nantucket.

---

* The article can be found in the Appendix.

16

The Pros Take Over

Were these athletes' lives, those of the Ironmen and their Princeton opposites, extraordinary? Certainly not in the context of the celebrity status that football heroes in later generations attained. Even though they played before big crowds, in games that brought big money to their colleges, they failed to see themselves as conquering heroes, as famous. "We were college boys playing a game," said Roscoe.

The picture-in-the-newspaper scene they had known began to change for their successors following World War II and not for the better. Pepper Constable, a big fan, faithfully attended Princeton games but after awhile, said his wife Betty, he often walked out of Palmer Stadium in disgust. It's plain to figure out why.

The 120th match, November 15, 1997, was contested at a one-time-only site, Giants Stadium in East Rutherford, New Jersey…a change of womb 45 miles northeast of Princeton.

The Tigers had no den that fall, Palmer Stadium having been torn down. "Before it fell down," said athletic director Gary Walters. Decades of rainwater had seeped betwixt the cement and steel of the U-shaped 1914 stadium, causing attrition that turned parts of it to hidden mush.

Walters' concept was to play the traditional game in a nearby famous football stadium, thus enticing a crowd. The wishful concept failed, the announced attendance of 7,500 being obviously generous.

The audience was so small and congregated so tightly that it was possible to tally heads with a touch of accuracy, which I did. Around 2,500. I did count each body in one section on the Princeton side which contained my grandson Will and his parents Carol and Rick Hamlin, both members of the Princeton class of 1977.

Will Hamlin was 10 years old that afternoon, as I had been in 1934. What he saw that day made no mark on him, for good reason. A dull game won by Princeton, 9-0, in a bare place and he was surrounded by 77,000 empty pews. The next day the Giants played the Arizona Cardinals there before an almost full house.

Where had everyone else gone, the Princeton and Yale parishioners for Kelley and Kazmaier?*

Attendance, like a thermometer, is presumed to be a measurement of the health of various events, from the ecclesiastical to the theatrical. The presumption follows that the value of the occasion is calibrated by the number of bodies in the building, in the stadium.

Even though Princeton and Yale lost two thirds of their in-house audiences in the 1960's, it would be folly to devalue the annual contest. Regardless of not being there, a bunch of people want to know who won, every second or third Saturday of November.

---

* Dick Kazmaier, the 1951 Heisman Trophy winner, tailback of Princeton's undefeated teams of 1950 and 1951 coached by Charles Caldwell.

Big shots. The collective endowments of Princeton and Yale at last look topped $20 billion. Or quiet people, like author and Princeton resident John McPhee. His father was the team doctor in the Caldwell Kazmaier era.

The downsizing of the congregation reflected a lot about the shifts in the American sports culture in the half century following 1934. Some of the factors are tangible ones…the automobile, coeducation, television…and some shadowy like the expansion of life's choices, or the intrusion of professional football. Whatever, the combination was effective.

College football was a major sports attraction through the Depression years and those following World War II. Then came television, and the tectonic plates moved.

That college football was a product that could be sold was long recognized by Princeton and Yale. Both had built big stadiums in 1914…Yale's a huge stadium…and in 1927 that university cleared a $1 million profit from the Elis' seven home games.

But neither institution wanted to be in the football entertainment business…*Beer & Circus*, as suggested by Murray Sperber, the Indiana University professor and author in 2000 of the book of that name. The creation of the Ivy League in 1954 was a statement endorsing the primacy of the educational mission by Brown, Columbia, Cornell, Dartmouth, Harvard, Pennsylvania, Princeton and Yale.

The National Collegiate Athletic Association, a somewhat toothless tiger founded in 1906, tried to control and share television's bounty in TV's early years but eventually failed. The major state universities with big-time football programs, along with some private universities like Notre Dame and Southern California, followed the money trail successfully.

The Ivies were shut out of network television, especially after the N.C.A.A. split major-college football into two divisions, I-A and I-AA, in 1981. Because the criterion was in part based on the capacity of stadiums, the Ivies were dumped into I-AA inasmuch as the facilities at Brown and Dartmouth lacked the minimum requirement of 30,000 seats. Each was about 10,000 short.

Stadium capacity was an excuse for a convenient removal. The Ivy League pests for decades had been barking at N.C.A.A.. conventions about sanity, reform, education, graduation…commentary which the big time athletic directors, like Michigan's Don Canham, did not wish to hear. Under Canham, the gross from Michigan's athletics had attained $16.5 million by 1989, $6.3 million of which came from television. Football…home games in a stadium seating 101,701…had a nice yield too.

And to think that Michigan had been an occasional Yale opponent, the last time in 1939.

Walter Byers, for 36 years the executive director of the N.C.A.A., wrote a book, *Unsportsmanlike Conduct,* in 1995 that more university presidents should have read. In it he commented, "The Ivy Group has done a far better job than any other major-college community in making the rules match their ideals.

"They held their ground despite the high publicity payoff and the enormous television revenues that went to other schools. The Ivies literally paid an athletics price for their principles. Everybody picked on them."

Princeton, Yale and the others got along without the television revenue quite nicely as their endowments testified, Yale's having reached $11 billion by 2004 and Princeton's

$8.5 billion. But the medium reduced their football patrons by a lot.

With the coming of cable television, the market diffused. There were as many as 20 college football games to be found on any television screen between Boston and New York on any Saturday, and seldom was a Yale game a choice. The same was true for Princeton, located in the equally saturated market between New York and Philadelphia.

Then there was pro football. In 1934 it was next to nothing as a competitor to college football…the Giants in New York or the Eagles in Philadelphia against Yale or Princeton games. By 1964 there no longer existed any thought of competition, the National Football League having established itself as the premier entertainment vehicle for the splendid American game.

The American football fan in search of a favorite team was far less inclined to pick a college one…unless an alumnus or a parent…than the heavily promoted NFL product so visible there on the television screen. Is it only a coincidence that the screen and the football field share the same rectangular shape?

The N.F.L.'s ascendancy began in the 1960's and was completed in the 1970's. Both Princeton and Yale helped…an incongruous druthers. Each gave their stadiums to the pros as sites to display the older, certainly better skilled athletes…although not necessarily better games.

(Who's to judge the better game? Or, as Red Smith wrote more than once, "Twelve-year-olds play this game too.")

Yale dove into compromise first when Bill Ford of The Fords, an alumnus and a significant Detroit Lions' stockholder, pulled the right Bulldog strings.

The heretofore sacrosanct Yale Bowl, the shrine to Walter Camp as "the father of football," was the site of a preseason exhibition game on September 11, 1960, between the Lions and the New York Giants. A crowd of 50,000 attended the insignificant event, which ended in a tie score, 16-16. The lion had penetrated the dog kennel.

Yale's take from that Sunday is hidden in obscure university financial files. But it was found money.

Princeton went next. Would Ken Fairman, '34, the bow-tied athletic director who had played the right end position with such distinction for Crisler, be amenable to a preseason exhibition game between the Giants and the Philadelphia Eagles since Yale had set the precedent? Of course.

The Eagles and the Giants had played an emotional series of games that counted in Philadelphia's Franklin Field and at New York's Yankee Stadium between 1959 and 1961. Why not add a third meeting each year, a preseason one, and where better than Palmer Stadium, halfway between the two cities?

By then Princeton crowds had begun to diminish, possibly because of the television options even though the teams of the remarkable Charlie Caldwell/Dick Colman coaching era were still winning ones.

Beginning in 1962 and ending in 1974, on a late August or early September afternoon, the Eagles and Giants played an N.F.L. preseason game in Palmer Stadium and usually the 49,000 seats were filled. The crowds were not of the college kind, more impolite and demanding of their teams.

As the automobiles by the hundreds came down the back roads out of New Brunswick the firemen from places along the way like Rocky Hill and Kendall Park held out plastic buckets seeking cash donations. Here was commerce.

Yale's pandering was to be more complete. The Bowl had been the site of other N.F.L. preseason games after 1960, the most notable the one matching the two New York teams for the first time in 1969, the defending Super Bowl champion Jets featuring their star, Broadway Joe Namath, against the pitiful Giants. The occasion was not an asset for Yale. The crowd was one of the largest ever, one beyond the counting of the 70,874 seats, and many never got there. All the roads were full up as every New Yorker with an interest in these two teams had taken a car and headed East-Northeast for Yale.

The grass on the floor of the Bowl was sparse and brown because of an unknown affliction, explained Yale spokesman Cappy Jones. Don Maynard, the pithy wide receiver for the Jets, spat and commented, "I've played on better high school fields in Texas."

The university, running deficits and searching for cash, rented out the Yale Bowl in 1973 and 1974 to the Giants, a team desperate for a home while its new stadium was being erected in the Meadowlands of New Jersey.

The pro team had 60,000 season-ticket buyers, plus a waiting list, and Yale Bowl had the most seats available because the Giants had been shut out of a temporary refuge, city-owned Shea Stadium, by Mayor John Lindsay who happened to be a Yale alumnus. After the Giants had signed a 30-year lease with the New Jersey Sports Authority in 1971, Lindsay thus retaliated in a political move designed to assuage the allegedly wounded feelings of New Yorkers.

Lindsay's successor, Abraham Beame, relented and let the Giants rent Shea Stadium in 1975. The next season the New York team was in New Jersey in a palace.

In the midst of the New York franchise's 15-year drought, these Giants teams at Yale lost 11 of 12 games, played before large but ugly crowds. The old bowl was shabby, the limited lavatory availability as impossible as in 1914, and the traffic choking. Yale never told how much rent the Giants paid. No amount could have been enough.

17

What Else Happened?

It is hard to assess just how much damage this propinquity to pro football did to the popularity of Princeton and Yale football. There certainly were a number of other factors, such as coeducation which commenced in 1969.

By 1975 half the undergraduate enrollments of each college, between 4,500 and 5,000, had suddenly become women, who were less inclined to spend Saturday afternoons going to a football game than were the men who in previous generations felt peer pressure to support their teams by their presence.

It has also been suggested that these enrollments now included many more students with ethnic backgrounds (Asian, for example) that had no football heritage.

Let us include the automobile. In 1934 Jim DeAngelis knew no one at Yale who had a car. If you wanted to go somewhere, you went by train or bus. Half a century later perhaps half the undergraduates had autos stashed in New Haven or Princeton. They could go anywhere any time.

Yale Bowl two-thirds full for Harvard game, 2001

It simply was no longer so necessary to go to the football game. That went for alumni too, especially at Princeton after Yale teams won their game 14 times in a row and 17 out of 18 times between 1967 and 1984. Yale being Yale, that really hurt and cost three head coaches their jobs…Jake McCandless, Bob Casciola and Frank Navarro. The alumni response seemed to be "why bother going?"

In the downstairs pub area of the Cottage Club, the esteemed undergraduate fraternity on Prospect Street, there were large photographic murals of some of the heroes of Princeton's fine teams of the late 1940's and early 1950's such as Ed Mead, Dick Kazmaier and George Sella. A senior retainer of the club told me in 1976, with a hint of sadness, "No one notices. No one even knows who they were."

An assembly of 50,000 people sat in the Yale Bowl in 1937 to watch the all-American halfback Clint Frank play his last game there, against Princeton, while rain poured. On a similar rainy afternoon 61 years later there were about 2,500 spectators in the Yale Bowl for the Princeton contest amid the sweep of 63,250 empty wooden bench seats.

Bill Stack, a Yale captain who had played in the 1937 match, had a comment. "People won't sit in the rain for a football game anymore. Not when there's a TV set at home as an alternative. Why should they? Let's face it, we Americans have gone soft."

If some comfort comes from popularity, then a crowd at a football game is rewarding to those attending. Those in attendance are more inclined to believe their effort has worth. Princeton tried hard to lure back its alumni, and the undergraduates, with the opening of an admirable new stadium in 1998, one with a seating capacity…27,500…little more than half that of its predecessor. Most significant was the reduction in the price of tickets, $6 for all seats and a dollar more for the Yale game in odd-numbered years.

The response? Luke warm. The home attendance for Princeton has been consistently just above the Ivy League median, about 10,000 per game with a tick every other season when Yale comes down and about 20,000 attend.

Then there is perception. Whatever is on television or in the newspapers is perceived as being important, right?

The Princeton-Yale football game lost an eyeball when in 1998, for the first time in the event's history, the New York *Times* did not personally attend the occasion. No staff sportswriter was assigned.

In my then almost 50 years of sportswriting, I believe I had written up at least 40 Princeton-Yale games, certainly more than any other event in my package for the *Times*.

An aside. After one game the former president of Colgate, Everett Case who was a Princeton alumnus, became so annoyed at my commentary he wrote a letter of complaint. I had not described the chronology of the game, won by Yale, but too much the heroics of the Yale running back who set records, Dick Jauron. Jim Roach, my sports editor then whom I adored, chided me. "Not one of your best, Bill," he said.

What was I assigned to do that day in 1998 when the *Times* rejected Princeton and Yale? I was given no assignment, sat in the stands and watched, quite contented.

The sports department at that time was somewhat chaotic, and the editor in charge of the Sunday sports section, the one recording college football of the previous day, was a young African American woman from Texas, new to the East. The premise that "all politics is local" had similarly applied to the paper's college football reportage...and everything else in sports...since forever because that was how to sell papers.

This editor went for the big picture. The *Times* was extolling itself as a national newspaper, and so the priority became the top 25 teams in the country. The demography of the *Times'* readers within the 200-mile circulation radius, where the bulk of the readers lived and bought, played no role. There were a lot of Princetons and Yalies out there in important places, making buying decisions having to do with the *Times*. No matter. Church and state are separate.

In lieu of a staff reporter writing up this game in 700 words, a rudimentary 150-word summary appeared in the *Times* as a part of a round-up of all four Ivy League contests with attribution to The Associated Press. The A.P. in turn got the information from stringers, meaning freelance operatives that the host team's sports information director could find. This resolution, with an occasional exception, has carried into the 21st century.

That first time it happened, a longtime Connecticut sportswriter commented, "The *Times* not covering a Princeton-Yale game? My god!"

Leadership didn't help. Neither Princeton nor Yale had presidents who were fans of football, and one, Yale's Bart Giamatti, gave a speech in 1980 that was widely interpreted as being anti football. Giamatti's passion for baseball…he later became major-league baseball's commissioner…had a short reach.

No matter the causes, this downsizing…or de-emphasis, as the chosen word became…did not sit well everywhere. The sight of an almost empty Yale Bowl…especially the almost empty sections reserved for the students…has bothered Bulldog boosters for decades.

When the wooden top rows of the Bowl were torn out in 1994, the capacity contracted by about 6,600 seats to 64,269. On occasion a Harvard game has attracted more than 50,000 spectators, but an assembly of more than 25,000 is a rarity, one of 15,000 common.

Nevertheless a defiant athletic director at Yale, Tom Beckett, has challenged diminishment with a series of aggressive marketing devices that have born fruit. Twice Yale has had the highest average game attendance of the 118 colleges in Division I-AA, 23,578 in 2003 and 29,347 in 1985.

Beckett's intention is to bring about a 21st century renovation of the Bowl by means of an investment of $20 million or more, in part to be funded by former players who have been targeted as primary contributors. Regardless of progressive alteration, empty pews will still stare.

There are occasional suggestions for more radical treatment. Why not shrink it…tear out a big chunk and leave an open end? Or fill this new empty space with a glitzy training facility, possibly to attract better football recruits?

Why not schedule more seductive opponents than, say, Dayton or San Diego, two recent foes, to pull more people into the Bowl?

The reply might be which ones? The professionalism in Division I-A precludes any "name" teams scheduling Yale. A bowl-game invitation is the goal for those teams, and an obstacle would be a game against Yale or any other Division I-AA opponent. Such matches (presumed victories) cannot count as one of the required six winning contests any I-A team needs to qualify for a bowl bid.

Princeton, Yale and the other Ivies are shackled to the football that they've got…that they inherited.

There is a lot to be said, however, for the undergraduate experience of being a player, wearing the uniform, in Princeton Stadium or Yale Bowl. Each team on these Saturdays will have as many as 100 players in uniform for home games even though only about 44 will actually participate…four times as many as in the afternoon of the Ironmen.

18

Larry Kelley

There were two Larry Kelleys. One was a luminary, created in part by the inventions of others that Kelley encouraged…or seldom denied. The other was a private man, quiet, questioning, searching, to the last day, when Lawrence Morgan Kelley took a pistol to his head.

Kelley's celebrity commenced that afternoon in Palmer Stadium when he scored the touchdown in bringing down the Tigers. His coaches and his teammates already knew how good he was from the previous six games. But the Ironmen match catapulted him into headlines.

He would play in 18 more games for Yale, 14 of them victories; be elected captain of the 1936 team; be voted all-American unanimously; and be awarded the newly named Heisman Trophy as college football's best player that season.*

His "life story" came out the following October in a two-part series in the *Saturday Evening Post*, the largest-circulation weekly in the country, with the title, "Everybody There Saw Kelley." The biography was written in first-person style

---

* The only other lineman ever voted a Heisman Trophy was another end, Leon Hart of Notre Dame in 1949.

under his name but the actual author had been his Boswell, George Trevor.

The sports archives at Yale grow in a big basement room in the Ray Tompkins House, the university's athletic administration headquarters, and the Kelley materials exceed those of any other athlete in this all-sports pantheon going back to the first intercollegiate competition, the Harvard-Yale crew race of 1852.

Captain Lawrence Morgan Kelley

Jim DeAngelis may not have been entirely correct when he said plaintively of the Ironmen, "No one remembers…But I do." Plenty remembered Larry Kelley when the auction of his Heisman Trophy in 1999 for $328,110 became a national Associated Press story 63 years after his last game. Or when he died six months later.

Kelley was born May 30, 1915, in Conneaut, Ohio, on the shore of Lake Erie at the Pennsylvania border. His family circumstances were modest and his father, he said, had shoveled iron ore on the Conneaut docks.

The father, a self-taught mechanical engineer, became an inspector of aircraft engines and that skill took the family first to to Chatham, Ontario, in 1917 and then for good to Williamsport, Pa., where the renowned Lycoming engines were made.

Kelley, in junior and senior high schools there, was mediocre in football but skilled as to high jumping and basketball. More important he was a good student, good enough to win a scholarship at Peddie, a modest prep school in Hightstown, N.J., eight miles from Princeton.

He placed first in his class of 67 boys and the Peddie football coach, a Yale alumnus named Earl MacArthur, encouraged him to try for New Haven. He was accepted and gained a regular scholarship which he needed.

On the freshman team he worked his way up from fifth string to first and in a losing match against Princeton he caught 11 straight passes, phenomenal for the time.

But Kelley was not a regular in his first varsity game, a loss against Columbia, the next autumn. However, he started the second half and caught a spectacular pass from Roscoe in the end zone for Yale's only score.

The myths began to build after the Ironmen's decision over Princeton. Many credited Kelley with the juicy remark to the Tiger captain following their fumbles, "Hey, Kadlic, does the Rose Bowl have handles on it?" But it was Grosscup.

Captain Lawrence Morgan Kelley

Trevor of the New York *Sun* was never above invention and he had the cheek, in the *Post's* autobiography, to have Kelley write, "This myth of Kelley, the all-American jester, needs to be debunked. It was all a conspiracy. Down in New York a Yale graduate, Gould Martin, thought up some of my best wisecracks and passed them on to sportswriters."

The harmless Martin, a stout little man who hung around the Yale Club a lot, had the ears of Joe Williams, the columnist for the *World-Telegram*, Dan Parker of the *Mirror* and some others.

Writing in sports was held to loose standards of accuracy, accountability. Exaggerations or falsehoods were taken lightly. No wonder the sports department of a newspaper was sometimes referred to as the toy department.

So a player for a Pennsylvania team, ahead by two touchdowns, was said to have said to Kelley, "I thought you were a gabby guy. You're awfully quiet today." His alleged retort: "Oh, do you fellows speak English?"

That was a low blow reflecting the number of players on the Penn squad with many consonants in their surnames. Did Kelley say it? No. Gould Martin did.

Kelley and fans, Hotel Taft's bar, New Haven, 1935

Trevor, a commuter who went home to Port Chester, N.Y., rather than the Yale Club, was never to be underestimated. Yet he was kindly and enthusiastic while overcoming an unsettling appearance…one walleye and drool coming from a corner of the mouth when George became excited.

Did Kelley, upon scoring a touchdown against Harvard in 1934, go up to an official, extend a hand and say, "I thought you might like to shake hands with me. Everybody else does." No, he did not.

Did he, in Philadelphia, say while looking aloft, "Well, I'm glad to see they know I'm in town." Kelley supposedly was commenting about an aerial sign being towed by an autogiro (predecessor of the helicopter) over Franklin Field, where the Penn-Yale game of 1935 was being played. The sign read, "Kelly For Mayor."

No, he did not say that.

He had just scored a touchdown that put Yale ahead and among his teammates he did point to the sign, saluting it with some glee. Running for mayor was John B. Kelly, the noted one-time oarsman, friend of Franklin D. Roosevelt, constructor of Federal buildings built with Kelly-made bricks. A Democrat, he lost.

Did Kelley accost the Harvard quarterback, Bob Haley, after the Yale end smeared a Crimson sweep for a loss, and say, "What kind of judgment you call that, Haley, trying Kelley's end on fourth down?" No, he did not.

In a 1936 game against Navy in Baltimore, the Midshipmen's Snead Schmidt fumbled on a punt return and there was a scramble. Kelley rushed in and the ball bounced off his foot or ankle, bounced all the way down to the Navy two-yard line where the famous Yale man downed it. First down, Yale. Clint Frank scored two plays later and the Bulldogs won, 12-7.

There was a hullabaloo. Had Navy been had? The rule stated that a ball kicked deliberately was dead at the spot but one kicked inadvertently continued in play. The field judge, Shorty Miller, ruled that it had been an accident and his decision stuck.*

---

* Because of that play, a change was made in the rules so it could not happen again.

Had the clever Kelley kicked the ball on purpose, as many supposed? “No,” he replied. “I’m not that smart.”

Yes, he did say that.

These smart remarks, in one fashion or another, were repeated and widely published. America’s sports followers cackled. That Yale fellow was quite a clown. And he got away with it too. Look at all the touchdowns he scored…he had 15 in 25 games which was a lot for an end in the 1930’s.

Kelley was also canny enough not to deny his wisecracks, not to set the record straight. He didn’t care, and neither did his teammates nor his coaches. Kelley could play.

Although Mac Farmer never said as much, the athletic director had to be delighted. Kelley’s prominence was helping to sell tickets and there were plenty to be had for the big Bowl.

The Yale hero was inclined to take it easy sometimes in afternoon practices whose repetitions bored him. Bill Beinecke, in his autobiography,* recalled an afternoon on Anthony Thompson Field when the junior varsity was attempting to demonstrate the plays of Saturday’s opponent to the varsity.

Beinecke, a jayvee, lined up opposite Kelley but not exactly in the right spot. Kelley reached across the scrimmage line, lifted Beinecke and moved him to the correct place, plopped the body down and said, “Stand over here, son.”

Exclaimed Beinecke, “And here I was a senior and he was an underclassman!”

---

* William S. Beinecke’s “Through Mem’r’ys Haze” recounted how he built an inherited company, Sperry and Hutchinson with its celebrated Green Stamps, into a trading-stamp behemoth.

Now there is a story we can embrace, the Kelley who had another kind of wit that stayed within the moment…not the public broadcast kind.

Greasy Neale, who could be expansive in a social setting and who had certainly appreciated Larry, said more than once that Jock Sutherland, an esteemed coach of strong will, "Would not stand for Kelley on his Pittsburgh teams for one minute! Not one minute!…Half the time Larry forgot to block…Princeton even had a play called the Cousin Kelley Special."

In the 1935 rout by the Tigers, the Cousin Kelley Special emerged. Princeton had a favored end-around play to its right, away from Kelley's position. It was noticed that the Yale man sensing such a play would quickly abandon his ground and cut across, trailing Tiger left end John Paul Jones so as to wreck his trick run.

So Pepper Constable faked the hand-off to Jones coming around, then whirled and pitched a lateral pass to Jack White going the other way. White sped past the flank left exposed by Kelley and scored from nine yards out. The Tigers scoffed. They had shut up that big Yale mouth

Kelley was by his admission a more interested offensive player than a defensive one. Defensive end play was a dicey business in the 6-2-2-1 scheme because the common off-tackle power plays were planned to sweep aside the end who had the choice of fighting off one or two blockers. Or crashing.

The latter meant zooming into the foe's backfield before the blocking could form and thus disrupting the play. There was risk. The crashing end could be swept aside by a trap block set by a pulling guard. He could be made inconsequential by a reverse play the other way. Or…horrors…by a deep double reverse like Columbia's feared and famous KF-79.*

Kelley liked to crash. As the right end he opposed the left side of the attacking team which, in the single-wing projections, wasn't the favored way to go. We are a right-handed culture, and the single-wing offense most often sent its power plays right. That is why Choo Choo Train played left end for Yale. He was much better at busting a play.

Kelley counted on Jack Wright…the right tackle, his best friend and roommate…to cover for him. And, in 1934, on right halfback Strat Morton to come up and cover too.

Yale, and Kelley, got even for the Princeton 1935 thrashing the next year in one of the more exciting games of the series. Clint Frank had come forth as a triple-threat tailback…runner, passer, blocker, plus a superb defensive diagnostician and tackler. Princeton had lost only to Penn, 7-0, Yale only to Dartmouth, 11-7, and a crowd of 57,000 overflowed Palmer Stadium.

The Tigers were ahead, 16-0, after Jack White scored the second of his two touchdowns. A touchdown by Frank made the halftime score, 16-7, and it was 16-14 after a 22-yard scoring run from Al Hessberg. Then, out of a spread formation, Kelley went deep into the secondary and Frank let go a 50-yard pass from his 25.

Kelley caught the pass and saw the swift White bearing down on him. The ingenious Bulldog turned and ran right at the Princeton man, attacking rather than fleeing. A sudden,

---

* Al Barabas scored the touchdown on that play in Columbia's 7-0 victory over Stanford in the 1934 Rose Bowl game. For football historians, knowing KF-79 became a test of the code…an admissions requirement.

savage stiff arm knocked White to the ground and Kelley ran to the end zone, putting Yale ahead for the first time, 20-16.

Princeton struck back and led, 23-20, only to have Yale score last to win, 26-23, on a stirring 13-yard run through traffic by Frank.

The generous Crisler said, "It was the most exciting game I've ever seen. If the teams could have gone on playing, it might have been 79-76. But Yale would have won."

The Kelley play was the most resourceful he had known. "That's what I call quick thinking under fire," said the Princeton coach. "Did you ever hear of a pass receiver attacking the tackler?"

Kelley told an interviewer almost 50 years later, "I turned toward him (White) and gave him a stiff arm, breaking his cheek and flipping him over. That was my revenge for the 'Kelley Special.'"

There was also lucky Larry. In the 1935 Harvard match a pass from Roscoe was a little short for Kelley, in between and covered by two backs, Fred Moseley and Tom Bilodeau. The ball caromed off Moseley's fingers, went through Bilodeau's arms and into Kelley's hands. He raced 30 more yards to the Harvard goal and Yale won, 14-7. Moaned Moseley, "I helped make him all-American."

In his final Yale game the following year, Harvard lost again, 14-13 this time, and the victors' second touchdown came on a 42-yard, fourth-down pass, Frank to Kelley. The Cantabs, the Crimson, were glad to see him go.

By then such was the Yale man's fame that Grantland Rice, the foremost syndicated sports columnist in the nation, wrote of him in verse, a frequent Rice contrivance:

If you figure they've overplayed fiction
Where Merriwells rise to the fray,
Without the least semblance of friction
And make the star play of the day.
If you figure such stuff is a breeder
Of yarns that are foolish or stale…
Just a moment, I beg of you, reader…
Shake hands with L. Kelley of Yale.

19

Fortunate Athletic Happenstance

L. Kelley of Yale had never heard of the Heisman Trophy and he wasn't alone. This award was the invention of a man named Bill Prince, an officer of the Downtown Athletic Club in New York City, and its purpose was to give publicity to the five-year-old organization, one saddled with debt and always needy of members.

Sportswriters would vote for college football's best player "East of the Mississippi," and the first recipient of the D.A.C. Trophy was Jay Berwanger, a running back for the University of Chicago. His uniform number was 99…"as close to a perfect 100 as I could get," explained his coach, Clark Shaughnessy.

Then John W. Heisman died the next year, in October. He was a retired football coach of some prominence and the athletic director of the D.A.C. who didn't think much of the award…which was promptly named after him, in his honor and memory.

The voting at the end of the 1936 season was expanded with ballots sent all over the country. Yale's Kelley, whose exploits on the field and quips on and off it had generated reams of copy, was voted the prize.

A telegram was dispatched to "Larry Kelley, Yale University." Western Union knew who he was. It read, "Sportswriters have voted you the outstanding football player in the United States and winner Heisman Memorial Trophy given by Downtown Athletic Club. Congratulations. W.B. Prince Chairman Trophy Committee."

"I didn't know there was such a thing," Kelley said later. A luncheon followed at the club in New York, not a dinner banquet, and Kelley responded to the moment. He knew his reputation required a jape and so he began his acceptance speech in this manner: "Fellow Rotarians." The audience roared.

It was a Wednesday. Rotarians nationwide had their luncheons on Wednesdays. Swift, that Kelley.

He also said, with an astonishing prescience, "Football today is a great business, as great as many of the businesses in which you are engaged. And two things have built it up: the press and the radio."

He went to many a banquet that winter,* attempting to please but not always succeeding. Art McGinley, the veteran Hartford Times sports writer attending one affair featuring Kelley, was sure a column would come of the evening. He went away disappointed. The Yale star didn't say anything funny, wrote McGinley.

Kelley played in the all-star East-West Shrine game on January 1 in San Francisco's Kezar Stadium, won by the East, 3-0, on a field goal by Princeton's Ken Sandbach.

---

* Perhaps the best was at the Lycoming Hotel in Williamsport. Headlines: "Home-Town folks pay tribute to their famous boy. He helped put Williamsport on the map." His parents and his sister were honored too.

Kelley was playing way out of position when he made a game-saving interception of a lateral pass and the West's coach, Babe Hollingbery of Washington State, scolded him afterward, "You'd never play for me."

Coach Kelley tapes his player's ankle at Peddie, 1937.

Kelley was not going to play for anyone. After graduation he went on a grand tour of Europe with five fun-loving classmates, one of whom was Potter Stewart who had been chairman of the Yale *Daily News* and the all-around ace of the Class of 1937. Stewart would become a notable Supreme Court justice.

In early September Kelley was the starting right end for the College All-Stars against the New York Giants in the *Herald Tribune's* Fresh Air Fund game in which he did nothing of note in his final, final game.

That fall found him back the Peddie School. He had taken an appointment for $2,000 a year as a teacher of history and mathematics and the successor to his old football coach, Earl MacArthur. This would be his career, he decided, and a few graduate classes over at Princeton were of some help.

The Detroit Lions drafted Kelley and offered an $11,000 contract. He wasn't interested, nor had been Choo Choo Train, Pepper Constable and Jack Weller, all drafted the year before, and Clink Frank the next year. "Pro football didn't have a good reputation back then," said Kelley.

He did, however, flirt with the Boston Shamrocks of the upstart American League in October, 1937. The team announced it had signed him to a contract and a good crowd of 7,500 turned out for a game in Fenway Park expecting to see the Yale Irishman in action. He begged off, saying he had influenza, and sat in the stands. "It was all blah, blah, blah," he said later.

Baseball? He had been a very good first baseman for Yale. The New York Yankees' scout, Paul Krichell, had made an offer. So had Branch Rickey of the St. Louis Cardinals. But Kelley backed off. "I guess I was scared of the major-league curve ball," he once explained.

Wall Street? "I had a lot of offers. I had no ambition that way. I didn't care about money."

Hollywood? Someone came up with a film scheme, "Kelley of Yale," with the real goods to play the title role. "I didn't think I could do it," he said, meaning he didn't want to bespatter himself.

Peddie was fine for Kelley. He stayed five years and along the way he married in September, 1939, Katherine Duncan by whom he had a daughter, Katherine Lynne, according to Yale alumni records. We know no more.

The Peddie basketball coach, Kink Sprout, told an interviewer: "Some people expected Larry to come down here and make a lot of noise and put on a big show. But he's not like that at all and the boys respect him for that. He kids them along and they like it."

Bill Wallace found Kelley at Peddie in the spring of 1941. I was just 17, a catcher for the junior varsity baseball team of The Hill, the prep school in Pottstown, Pa., which regarded Peddie as a distant third relative to its prime rivals, Hotchkiss and Lawrenceville.

Whereas the varsities played on the premier diamond, the jayvees were on a faraway field. Peddie, the host, had to supply the umpires. While warming up my pitcher, Bill Manierre, I saw the single umpire taking his place behind the pitching mound from where he would adjudicate all decisions, including balls and strikes.

Good heavens, that's Larry Kelley.

I vaguely remembered he was at Peddie and, as a Yale Bowl boy, I recognized the person now in shirt sleeves and casual khaki trousers.

Jayvee games are painfully unimportant, easily dismissed. My pitcher was wild as usual and I did my best. I jerked his pitches right to left into the strike zone. Lo, Kelley, standing 65 feet away, was calling strikes.

I kept it up. I think we won.

Clint Frank, Yale President Bart Giamatti, Kelley,
Heisman Trophy donation event, 1981.

Bill Wallace recounted this episode to Larry Kelley the one time we met, in 1981 at a Yale football luncheon before a Harvard game. I was there as a newspaperman, a reporter. I would test his alleged humor, poke at the famous Kelley.

"You were my hero," I said. "I had such guilt. Getting strikes that were balls."

We were alone for a moment. Kelley smiled and said, "Well, if you hadn't done that, we'd all still be out there."

Perfect. I had the right hero.

The war misdirected him. He failed to pass physical examinations for the Navy on account of perforated ear drums or some such. Swept up by war's impulses he abandoned teaching and worked in a defense industry, as a manager for the Lawrence Aeronautical Corporation in Linden, N.J.

In March 1946 he was married again, to Anne Goodwin according to Yale records, and moved to Gloversville, N.Y., where he worked for a company that made gloves, of course. He continued in that line of business for firms in Reading, Pa., and Glens Falls, N.Y., for 12 more years.

Then in 1958 he went back to teaching and coaching at Cheshire Academy in Cheshire, Conn. For the 25th reunion class book he wrote, "It was a great relief to return to the academic pastures, where I was recently joined by a childhood sweetheart." The latter was Lovdie Augusta Welsh, and they were married on July 22, 1961, in St. Petersburg, Fla.

Kelley was at Cheshire for 12 years and then returned to Peddie as director of alumni affairs for five years until his retirement in 1975.

In 1969 Kelley was voted into the college football Hall of Fame and said he was "flattered" even though he had waited a long time. "I thought I'd be a bridesmaid forever," he said.

Back in Hightstown he became reacquainted with Gerome (Red) Becker who had been a friend before the war and who had served as the town's mayor, postmaster and head of the board of education. Larry remembered from back then Red's sister, Mary Ruth, who now had just retired from the Navy, with rank of a Commander after an impressive 30-year career in the nursing field.

They met again, connected, and married in 1975, then chose to live their retirements in Pensacola, Fla. From there Kelley said to Pat Harmon of the Cincinnati *Post*, "I cut the grass and hit the golf ball. I cut the grass better than I hit the golf ball."

The couple were in Pensacola for 16 good years and then returned to Hightstown, to a pleasant house on Orchard Avenue a block from the school. They were home at last.

Bill Stack, Yale's 1939 football captain, had said of Kelley, "Larry certainly marched to a different set of drums." It was an authentic cliché, especially for Yale where this football star alternated in being conventional and rebellious.

After the Ironmen's football season he soon quit the basketball team because of a squabble with the coach, Elmer Ripley, who would not include him in the starting five. But he rejoined the team as a junior and senior.

He and Jack Wright pledged the fraternity Delta Kappa Epsilon but both resigned in protest after being paddled on the butt in the initiation ceremonies. "Childish" and "humiliating" were their words. But a year later they recanted and joined DKE.

Clint Frank, whose room was near that of Kelley and Wright in Trumbull College, said Kelley "always had the radio on" and never seemed "to crack a book." Yet he was an honor student just short of the Phi Beta Kappa level; a member of the Board of Control of the Undergraduate Athletic Association, the Budget Advisory Committee and the Senior Prom committee; head of the Class Day committee at graduation; and the last man tapped for Skull and Bones, symbolic of being the numero uno in his class.

Wright, who played next to him for three seasons, said he never heard Kelley say anything on the field. "He was all business."

Kelley told an interviewer 30 years later: "I had a great deal of self-confidence. In fact, immeasurable. But I didn't come on strong and I didn't go around bragging...I wasn't too serious. I didn't fit the Yale tradition. Back then athletes weren't supposed to say anything."

One quarter century out of college Kelley had turned humble. He wrote these sweet sentences for the Class of 1937's reunion book. "I fully enjoyed my undergraduate life and have a full and happy recollection of the privileges which were accorded me because of my fortunate athletic happenstance.

"While there were some occurrences which do not reflect well, I feel they were a part of the picture, and I do not really regret them...it has led to a full life...not a glorious one, nor one marked by achievement, as it is usually measured, but in my own fashion I am content...and full. For which I bless Mother Yale or Father Eli."

Herman Gundlach, Harvard's 1934 captain, and Kelley in Yale's Coxe Cage before H-Y game of 1985. Choo Choo Train peeking from behind.

Another quarter of a century later he had turned bitter and conservative, like Choo Choo Train. Yale had gone to pot, sports were discouraged and women undergraduates didn't belong there. Train and Kelley had stayed in touch, the former always signing off as TOE, which stood for The Other End.

When classmate Jack Field came down to Pensacola in 1986, on tour in preparing his two-volume class history called *Rendezvous With Destiny*,* Kelley was cordial. But he would not sit still for an interview. "I've got a golf date I can't break," he told the furious Field.

What was he hiding? Field guessed it had to do with Kelley not serving in the armed forces during World War II, that he was discomfited and didn't want to talk about the past.

He did fill out a questionnaire in which he wrote, "I adjusted to retirement with consummate ease, since I have been for long time principally lazy and largely devoid of ambition." He had also become plump, a big man weighing 230 pounds or more.

Mary Ruth Kelley, his widow who adored him, acknowledged: "Larry was definitely his own man and spoke his thoughts without reservation. At times those who did not know him well may have found him a bit blunt."

He never returned to New Haven for those June class reunions every five years. But he did come back for the three Ironmen reunions, at Princeton weekends in New Haven in 1974, 1984 and 1994. Kelley was also a dedicated member and a director of the Heisman Trophy Foundation, being present in New York every December for the awards dinner. The Foundation in turn held a dinner in his honor in 1990.

Health issues commenced. A concerned Kelley got the idea of linking his fame to funds by selling his last Heisman

---

* Field had played freshman football with Kelley and was a jayvee member for a while. His fine Yale book can be found sometimes on internet sites such Amazon.com.

Trophy. This schoolmaster had never earned enough money to build an estate of consequence.

There were at least two Heisman Trophies that passed through his hands, something which the foundation permitted. You could have a second, but not a third.

One he gave to Yale in 1981, as did Clint Frank* at a fancy ceremony featuring both gallants the day before the Harvard game. In the grand President's Room at Woolsey Hall, Kelley stood before a distinguished football audience and said, "I've had this little friend here for 45 years. It's been a good friend and an inspiration. I've patted it so often that the headgear is starting to wear off."

Yale would put the two trophies on prominent display. Kelley added, "I feel that if one or two potential Rhodes Scholars who happen to be able to run with the ball are inspired to come to Yale, it will serve its purpose."

His second Heisman Trophy was sold at Leland's auction house in New York on December 2, 1999, for $328,110, an unexpectedly high amount. It amused Kelley that his trophy had sold more for almost $100,000 more than that of O.J. Simpson a few years before.

Kelley had explained publicly, "I'm 84 and not doing too good, so I decided to let go all my memorabilia." He wished to put his affairs in order and leave something for nieces and nephews. These were all on his fourth wife's side of the family and there were 18 of them plus 24 grand nieces and nephews, according to Mary Ruth Kelley.

The Kelleys befriended the buyers, James and Terri Walsh, who had recently opened a restaurant, a sports bar called The Stadium in Garrison, N.Y., 30 miles north of New York City.

---

* Frank was voted the trophy in 1937.

It became a big success, thanks in part to a vast display of sports memorabilia.

Kelley had had open-heart surgery. "Then it was one thing after another," Mary Ruth Kelley told me one August day in 2003 when I dropped by the cheerful house on Orchard Avenue. "Several small strokes, carotid surgeries, new medicines. The doctors couldn't do anything for him. He had breathing problems and was depressed, discouraged.

"But never for a minute did I think."

She broke off and then told me that on Tuesday, June 27, 2000, she stepped out of the house for a few minutes.

"When I came back it was quiet. I called and there was no answer. That's strange, I thought. He was fine when I left. Then I saw the cellar door was open. My heart sank."

She had forgotten about the pistol that Larry had kept in a drawer against her wishes. "I'd asked him to get rid of it. He said he would."

Kelley had gone down the cellar stairs and shot himself in the basement. She found him there.

"He didn't want to be a burden," she said.

I was curious to know if the Kelleys were aware that Pepper Constable, the honored Princeton foe, had taken his life 13 years before by swimming into the ocean. But I didn't ask.

This social historian, of football and Yale, sometimes wishes he'd had the opportunity to know Larry Kelley…beyond our one chat at the Heisman Trophies-to-Yale luncheon with Clint Frank in 1981.

But that was good enough.

I had introduced myself by saying that I was a New York *Times* writer and such was all his fault.

I had been present at the Ironmen game in Princeton and it had inspired me to become a sportswriter.

His response?

"I forgive you."

Bibliography

Books:

Football Facts and Figures, Dr. L.H. Baker, Farrar & Rinehart, 1945.

History of Yale Football, Dr. L.H. Baker, unpublished, Yale Athletic Association, 1947.

The Game, Thomas Bergin, Yale University Press, 1994.

Football: The Ivy League Origins of An American Obsession, Mark F. Bernstein, University of Pennsylvania Press, 2001.

Unsportsmanlike Conduct: Exploiting College Athletes, Walter Byers, University of Michigan Press, 1995.

The Yale Football Story, Tim Cohane, G.P. Putnam' Sons, 1951.

Great College Football Coaches of the Twenties and Thirties, Tim Cohane, Arlington House, 1973.

The History of American Football, Allison Danzig, Prentice-Hall, 1957.

Rendezvous With Destiny. A History of the Yale Class of 1937 and Its Times, John W. Field, Phoenix, 1984.

Ivy League Autumns, Richard Goldstein, St. Martin's Press, 1996.

Tournament of Roses, Rick Hamlin, McGraw-Hill, 1988.

History of the Yale Class of 1936, John Hersey, et al. Yale University 1936.

Ivy League Football Since 1872, John McCallum, Stein & Day,1972.

Anatomy of A Game, David M. Nelson, University of Delaware Press, 1994.

A Yale Book of Numbers: Historical Statistics of The College and University, 1701–1976, George W. Pierson, Yale University Press 1983.

The Heisman, Anthology, William N. Wallace et al., Adventure Quest Inc., 1995.

College Football: History, Spectacle, Controversy, John Sayle Watterson, John Hopkins University Press, 2000.

Yale 1936 Fifty Years Out, Yale University.

Thirty Years Out-Class of 1936, Yale University.

Football Y Men, 1920–1939. Yale University Press 1963.

Periodicals: New Haven *Journal-Courier,* New Haven *Register*, New York *Herald Tribune*, New York *Times,* New York *Sun*, *Saturday Evening Post*, Princeton *Alumni Weekly*, Yale *Alumni Weekly*, Princeton and Yale Football Programs, 1934–1936.

Appendix

Play-by-Play and Statistics
George Trevor's Game Story
Betty Howe Constable on Pepper
By-Line Biographies

Statistics of The Game

Palmer Stadium, Princeton, N.J., November 17, 1934

Play-by-Play

A consensus from these disagreeing sources: Princeton and Yale Alumni Weekly magazines, New York Herald Tribune and New York Times.

First Quarter

Team
Possession Down & Yds. Yd.-Line Play

Curtin Y kick-off out of bounds.

Curtin Y kick-off to P end zone. Sandbach runback 1 yd. Tackled by DeAngelis.

P 1-10 @ P 1 LeVan punts to P 40. Roscoe returns 10.

Y 1-10 @ P 30 P offside. Penalty.
Y 1-10 @ P 25 Y offside. (Roscoe pass to Kelley incomplete.)
Y 1-10 @ P 30 Whitehead 8 on reverse.
Y 2-2 @ P 22 Y offside. (Roscoe pass to Kelley incomplete.)
Y 2-7 @ P 27 Fuller 1.
Y 3-6 @ P 26 Roscoe pass intercepted by Kalbaugh, returns 24.

P 1-10 @ Y 48 Constable 1.
P 2-9 @ Y 47 Constable fumble, Whitehead recover.

Y 1-10 @ Y 44 Morton 1.
Y 2-9 @ Y 45 Whitehead 1.
Y 3-8 @ Y 46 Fuller punts 54 to P end zone. Touchback

P 1-10 @ P 20 LeVan 3.
P 2-7 @ P 23 Sandbach 3.
P 3-4 @ P 26 LeVan 4.
P 1-10 @ P 30 Constable 3.
P 2-7 @ P 33 LeVan 4.
P 3-3 @ P 37 Constable 1.
P 4-2 @ P 38 LeVan punt partially blocked by Grosscup/ Scott. Out of bounds at Y 46.

Y 1-10 @ Y 45 Whitehead 6.
Y 2-4 @ P 49 Whitehead 3.
Y 3-1 @ P 46 Whitehead no gain.
Y 4-1 @ P 46 Fuller punt to P end zone. Touchback.

P 1-10 @ P 20 LeVan fumble, recover, loss of 3.
P 2-13 @ P 17 Sandbach 1.
P 3-13 @ P 18 LeVan punt 30, Morton return 2.

Y 1-10 @ P 46 Morton 3.

Y 2-8 @ P 43 Morton loss of 5.

Y 3-12 @ P 48 Roscoe pass 23 to Kelley who runs 25 for touchdown at 12:22. Curtin's conversion kick good. Yale 7 Princeton 0.

Curtin Y kicks off out of bounds.

Curtin Y kicks off to Sandbach who returns 26 to P 28.

P 1-10 @ P 28 Sandbach 3.

P 2-7 @ P 31 LeVan fumble, Fuller Y recover.

Y 1-10 @ P 33 Roscoe pass incomplete.

Y 2-10 @ P 33 Roscoe pass incomplete.

Y 3-10 @ P 33 Whitehead no gain.

Y 4-10 @ P 33 Fuller punts to end zone. Touchback.

P 1-10 @ P 20 LeVan 1.

P 2-9 @ P 21 LeVan 1.

Second Quarter

P 3-8 @ P 22 MacMillan punt 54, Roscoe return 6.

Y 1-10 @ Y 30 Whitehead 9.

Y 2-1 @ Y 39 Morton no gain.

Y 3-1 @ Y 39 Fuller punt 31

P 1-10 @ P 30 LeVan 2.

P 2-8 @ P 32 MacMillan 5.

P 3-3 @ P 37 LeVan 6 on lateral from MacMillan.

P 1-10 @ P 43 Sandbach 2.

P 2-8 @ P 45 Sandbach 5.

P 3-3 @ 50 MacMillan punt 7 out of bounds at Y 43.

Y 1-10 @ Y 43 Roscoe pass incomplete.
Y 2-10 @ Y 43 Roscoe pass intercepted by MacMillan.

P 1-10 @ Y 43 Sandbach pass incomplete.
P 2-10 @ Y 43 Constable 5.
P 3-5 @ Y 38 Spofford fumble lateral, Wright Y recover.

Y 1-10 @ Y 46 Whitehead no gain.
Y 2-10 @ Y 46 Roscoe 6.
Y 3-4 @ P 48 Roscoe 3.
Y 4-1 @ P 45 Fuller punt 25 out of bounds.

P 1-10 @ P 28 Kadlic pass incomplete.
P 2-10 @ P 28 MacMillan 2.
P 3-10 @ P 30 LeVan 46, tackle by Train.
P 1-10 @ Y 24 Kadlic loss of 5.
P 2-15 @ Y 29 LeVan pass to MacMillan 5.
P 3-10 @ Y 24 LeVan pass to MacMillan 19.
P 1-G @ Y 5 LeVan no gain.
P 2-G @ Y 5 Spofford 3, tackle by DeAngelis.
P 3-G @ Y 2 Constable no gain, tackle by Grosscup.
P 4-G @ Y 2 Spofford loss of 2, tackle by Grosscup.

Y 1-10 @ Y 4 Roscoe 3.
Y 2-7 @ Y 7 Roscoe 3.
Y 3-4 @ Y 10 Fuller punt 20, Spofford return minus 6, tackle by Train.

P 1-10 @ Y 36 Kaufman 5.
P 2-5 @ Y 31 Kaufman 4.

P 3-1 @ Y 27 Constable 4.
P 1-10 @ Y 23 Constable pass incomplete.
P 2-10 @ Y 23 Kadlic pass incomplete.
P 3-10 @ Y 23 Kadlic pass incomplete.

Third Quarter

Kadlic P kick-off to end zone, Roscoe returns 10.
Y 1-10 @ Y 10 Whitehead no gain.
Y 2-10 @ Y 10 Fuller punts 61.

P 1-10 @ P 29 Kaufman 9.
P 1-1 @ P 38 Constable 8.
P 1-10 @ P 46 LeVan 16.
P 1-10 @ Y 38 LeVan 6.
P 2-4 @ Y 32 LeVan 2.
P 2-2 @ Y 30 Constable 18.
P 1-10 @ Y 12 LeVan 5.
P 2-5 @ Y 7 Kaufman loses 3.
P 3-6 @ Y 10 LeVan pass incomplete.
P 4-6 @ Y 8 Kadlic pass to MacMillan out of bounds, touchback.

Y 1-10 @ Y 20 Morton 2.
Y 2-8 @ Y 22 P offsides.
Y 2-3 @ Y 27 Whitehead no gain.
Y 3-3 @ Y 27 Fuller punt 42, LeVan return 14.

P 1-10 @ Y 44 Constable 1.
P 2-9 @ Y 43 Kadlic pass incomplete.
P 3-9 @ Y 43 MacMillan punt 23. Roscoe no return.

Y 1-10 @ Y 20 P offsides.

Y 1-5 @ Y 25 Whitehead no gain.
Y 2-5 @ Y 25 Whitehead no gain.
Y 3-5 @ Y 25 Fuller punt 51. Pauk no return.

P 1-10 @ P 24 Kaufman no gain.
P 2-10 @ P 24 MacMillan 5.
P 3-5 @ P 29 Kadlic no gain.
P 4-5 @ P 29 MacMillan punt 41, Roscoe return 12.

Y 1-10 @ Y 42 Morton 6.
Y 2-4 @ Y 48 Fuller punt 30, out of bounds P 22.

P 1-10 @ P 22 Kaufman 2.
P 2-8 @ P 24 Pauk 1.
P 3-7 @ P 25 Constable no gain.
P 4-7 @ P 25 MacMillan punt 28. Roscoe return 5.

Y 1-10 @ P 48 Roscoe pass to Kelley 10.
Y 1-10 @ P 38 Whitehead 2.

Fourth Quarter

Y 2-8 @ P 36 Roscoe 2.
Y 3-6 @ P 34 Roscoe pass to Kelley 10.
Y 1-10 @ P 24 Morton 1.
Y 2-9 @ P 23 Roscoe pass incomplete.
Y 3-9 @ P 23 Curtin field goal attempt wide. Touchback.

P 1-10 @ P 20 MacMillan punt 42. Roscoe fair catch.

Y 1-10 @ Y 38 Morton no gain.
Y 2-10 @ Y 38 Morton 5.
Y 3-5 @ Y 43 Roscoe pass to Train 11.

Y 1-10 @ P 46 Whitehead lose 1.
Y 2-11 @ P 47 Fuller punt 37. LeVan return 33.

P 1-10 @ P 43 MacMillan pass intercepted. Fuller return 20.

Y 1-10 @ P 31 Morton lose 1.
Y 2-10 @ P 32 Fuller 4.
Y 3-5 @ P 28 Roscoe no gain.
Y 4-7 @ P 28 Fuller punt out of bounds P 2.

P 1-10 @ P 2 MacMillan punt 35, Roscoe return 2.

Y 1-10 @ P 33 Morton 2.
Y 2-8 @ P 31 Morton no gain.
Y 3-8 @ P 31 Whitehead 4.
Y 4-4 @ P 27 Fuller punt out of bounds P 3.

P 1-10 @ P 3 MacMillan punt 42, Roscoe return 20.

Y 1-10 @ P 25 Whitehead no gain, P penalty 15 roughing.
Y 1-10 @ P 10 Roscoe 2.
Y 2-8 @ P 8 Whitehead 1.
Y 3-7 @ P 7 Fuller no gain.
Y 4-7 @ P 7 Curtin field goal attempt wide. Touchback.

P 1-10 @ P 20 Sandbach pass incomplete.
P 2-10 @ P 20 Sandbach pass intercepted by Whitehead P 28.

Y 1-10 @ P 28 Whitehead no gain.

Team Statistics	**Yale**	**Princeton**
First Downs	3	8
Attempts & Yds. Rushing	40 for 71	43 for 185
Completed Passes	6 of 13 for 79	2 of 13 for 24
Intercepted by	2	2
Lost fumbles	0 of 1	3 of 8
Punts and avg.	13 for 43	11 for 39
Kick-return yards	71	27
Penalties	2 for 10	5 for 35

Individual Statistics

Rushing…Yale: Whitehead 18 for 35 yds.; Roscoe 7 for 19; Morton 12 for 14; Fuller 3 for 5. Princeton: LeVan 15 for 96; Constable 10 for 43; Kaufman 6 for 19; Sandbach 5 for 14; MacMillan 3 for 12; Spofford 3 for 0; Pauk 1 for 1.

Passing…Yale: Roscoe 6 of 13 for 79 yds., 2 intercepted, 1 touchdown. Princeton: LeVan 2 of 3 for 24; Sandbach 0 of 3, 1 intercepted; MacMillan 0 of 1, 1 intercepted; Kadlic 0 of 5; Constable 0 of 1.

…………	1	2	3	4	F
Princeton	0	0	0	0	0
Yale	7	0	0	0	7

Officials: W.T. (Bill) Halloran, Providence College, referee; Tom Thorp, Columbia, umpire; Lou Young, Pennsylvania, linesman; J.E. (Jim) Keegan, Springfield College, field judge.

Attendance---53,000.

Elis Boast Eleven Iron Men

By George Trevor
(New York *Sun*, Monday, November 19, 1934)

Scene one is the interior of the concrete locker building reserved for visiting teams just beyond the the gateway of Palmer Stadium at Princeton; time, 1:45; the Yale squad, only twenty-eight strong, has just trooped in after warming up.

Head Coach Raymond Pond, stocky, ruddy-faced, square-jawed, stands at the door leading from the locker quarters to the team room. "Regulars, this way!"

Pond clips off his words brusquely. "Step forward as I call your names: Train, Scott, Curtin, DeAngelis, Grosscup, Wright, Kelley, Roscoe, Whitehead, Morton"…there is a pause…"Fuller!"

The last named blinks his surprise. Rankin, whose place Fuller takes, merely tightens his lips. Cleated shoes clatter like wooden sabots an the floor. Shoulder harness creaks. The door slams. Pond is alone with this team.

"I didn't bring you here to make a speech." His voice is vibrant with repressed emotion. "You men know what kind of a job this is. You've got to stick in there for sixty minutes. Eleven men are going to start and finish this game No one leaves the field as long as he can stay on his feet."

Scene Two. The kickoff in Palmer Stadium: a perfect Indian summer afternoon; not an empty seat; concrete slopes covered with a human blanket, the colors soft and crooked like those of a hook rug.

Yale is grim and poised; Princeton is tense and jittery, the 5 to 1 favorite shoulders a heavy psychological burden. The Tigers have everything to lose. They've had easy sailing all season. For Yale, this is just another game in a blood and iron schedule. They've been through the mill.

Giant Captain Curtin, the one Eli who bulks as large as his burly foes, drives his foot against the ball. It soars into the end zone. Sophomore Ken Sandbach has only to touch it down or let it go to get twenty yards for Princeton. Instead he fumbles the ball, juggles it around. and finally scrambles out to the one-yard-line. Fortunately for the Elis they miss their end zone tackles and thus automatically escape making Princeton a present of nineteen yards.

Here is the keynote of the game. It reveals Princeton as strung tighter than a base drum, unable to relax and be itself. Tension is the thief of form. Seven Princeton fumbles tell the story of tiger tautness.

Scene three. Enter a wisecracking guy named Larry Kelley from Williamsport, Pa., and Peddie Prep, wearing a cocky grin on his Irish map. This Kelley is too good and doesn't care who knows it. Like Tom Shevlin, he talks a great game and then goes out and plays it. Kelley has just told reporters, that "Princeton's backfield won't look so smooth with me in it all afternoon"; he adds: "Ten minutes of Kelley and those Tigers will think they're playing Minnesota; Yale is going to win by two touchdowns, and I'll bag 'em both."

A shrinking violet, eh? Well, listen to this. Yale's ball on Princeton's 43-yard line; third down, twelve to go; kick formation; Fuller back. It's a fake. Roscoe grabs a short snap from center and fades two paces. Flippo! He wings a center-alley toss to Kelley who is striding free on Princeton's 29 yard stripe. It's just beyond Larry's reach…wow!…did you see him skyrocket aloft and collar that ball with one prehensile paw? A Honus Wagner grab!

Kelley juggles the slim-nosed pigskin momentarily, stows it under his left arm and lengthens his rakish stride as he veers toward the west sideline. The omnipresent Whitehead spills Kalbaugh. Kelley outruns Kadlic who vainly dives for his bright blue legs. Skirting the boundary Larry appears cornered at the 10 yard stripe by Constable and John.

Then, as a raindrop trickling down a window pane, pauses for a moment and spurts ahead. Kelley breaks his stride, stops dead, allows his foes to tackle empty air and cuts inside them. Le Van himself couldn't have done it more neatly.

Now Kelley sees the green pastures ahead. He gathers himself like a hurdler and and runs right through the clutching arms of Sandbach and Le Van.

"He's ovah!" claims the radio broadcaster. So he is, and standing up at that with a grin that reaches from one Kelley ear to the other.

Scene four: Le Van is loose and chills play tag down the spines of Yale partisans. As a shuttle weaves across a loom, so does the Steubenville Spook sift through a broken field, slipping tackler after tackler. This is the moment anticipated by Princeton and dreaded by Yale. Gary's nimble feet are kicking the chalk marks behind…ten, twenty, thirty, forty…it's Slagle's run all over again!

Who's this flashing like a blue comet across the cleat-bitten turf? Robert Train of Savannah, Ga., suh! Away down on Yale's 24-yard mark he rides Le Van to earth as a cowhand bulldogs a steer.

Scene five: A Princeton pass has clicked and the Elis dig in on their own five-yard mark while the crowd chants the time honored "Hold 'em Yale!" It seems that nothing can stop

Princeton power, but behind that thin blue line there rises a spectral barrier.

Of itself this Yale line must be overpowered by Tiger brawn. but behind each of Captain Curtin's men looms a phantom figure. They cannot see these shadowy shapes any more than you can but they can feel their presence. You who have imagination may picture tight-lipped Gordon Brown standing at Grosscup's elbow; you may visualize swashbuckling Jim Hogan lending supernatural power to Scott's charge; and lambent Stub Chamberlain reinforcing Wright's patrol.

From somewhere out of the dim past, this Yale line that has been ripped asunder in midfield finds the psychic strength to repulse the bludgeoning Constable and the juggernauting Spofford. It can't be done, but it is done! On second down Spofford rumbles tractor fashion to the one-yard mark. Constable butts his head against a blue wall and Kadlic stakes everything on the irresistible force that is Spofford. Before the latter can work up momentum Grosscup bullets through like a bat out of hell to halt the battering ram as the whole blue line surges forward in concert. Life has few such moments.

Scene six: It is the second half and Princeton is on the rampage. Seven rushes sweep the ball sixty yards toward Yale's goal. Constable is piledriving off the tackle like a Ted Coy. The Elis have their backs to the wall again. This time Kadlic resorts to aerial warfare instead of an artillery barrage. If he can't go through he will go over. His second end zone heave makes connections but alas for Princeton, MacMillan is just beyond the sideline as his eager fingers grip the ball. Up in Section 24, row 36, Pie Way, hero of the 1915 Yale rally, digs his nails into his palms and bites his cigar in two. A narrow squeak!

Scene seven: Kelley has won the game, but it takes Stan Fuller to save it. Kelley, the egotist, flaunts a superiority complex; Fuller, the introspective brooder, has been fighting down inhibitions bred of premature newspaper ballyhoo.

Since last spring he has been reading Roy Mills's book on control kicking and has practiced oblique punts. With a lead to protect as the last quarter wanes, Yale calls on Fuller to kick the Tiger into coffin corner. All afternoon, Fuller has been angling his punts out of Le Van's reach. He can drop that ball on a spot. Twice his low grasshoppers have saved Yale's goal. Now Stan demonstrates that the punt is an offensive weapon. Holding the ball in the Mills' manner, he twice punts out of bounds a yard from the Tiger end zone. Those oblique kicks nail down Princeton's coffin.

Scene eight: The Yale Club, New York city. A brass band hired in the morning (sublime optimism!) parades down Park avenue to the Princeton Club blaring "Bingo," "Boola" and "Down The Field." Johnny Woodruff has the "foreman's blackboard" bearing the legend "Yale 7, Princeton 0". Al Simmons leads the delirious Elis in a long cheer for Curtin's eleven ironmen; for Trainer Frank Wandle who conditioned them; for Coach Pond who endowed them with his unbeatable spirit.

Voices are raised in lusty refrain; tears trickle unabashedly down Yale cheeks; through the haze of tobacco smoke one can see the elms brooding over Old Brick Row; the initial-frescoed tables at Mory's; the knife-scarred fence around South Middle. The song swells in a crescendo!

Mother of men grown strong in giving
Honor to them thy light hath led;
Rich in the toil of thousands living

Brave in the deeds of thousands dead.
Thee whom our fathers loved before us.
Thee whom our sons unborn shall hail.
Praise we today in sturdy chorus
Mother of men—old Yale.

Pepper's Last Victory

Princeton Alumni Weekly, January 28, 1987
The Story of an Alzheimer's Disease Victim
By Betty Howe Constable

"When the day comes and I have lost my brain, I hope I'll have enough sense to end my life."

Those words were spoken by my husband, Pepper Constable, in the winter of 1981. A few months earlier, after much deliberation, he had diagnosed himself as a victim of Alzheimer's Disease and went, without my knowledge, to a neurologist to confirm his suspicions. Then he asked to be retired as director of health services at E.R. Squibb. The corporate medical director didn't believe it was true, but after seeing reports from two specialists, he realized that Pepper's diagnosis was correct.

Pepper had already told me that Alzheimer's was an "irreversible deterioration of the brain," but I called the neurologist and asked him to tell me exactly what to expect. He said, "Well, he'll end up as a vegetable in a nursing home."

That winter, for the most pat, Pepper seemed fine. He did sometimes forget the names of some very common things, but the most glaring effect was his inability to add, subtract, or divide the simplest of numbers. He had himself tested and when he was asked to subtract 7 from 100, he could not give an answer. I got him some grade school arithmetic workbooks to help him fight this problem, but that only made him feel more inadequate. I also noticed that he had coins all over the house—it turned out he was paying for everything with paper money because he could not make change.

From the beginning I wanted everyone to know about my husband's illness. There was no way to tell how fast the disease would destroy his brain. If he should get lost or say or do something unlike himself, I wanted our friends to help us out and to protect him with understanding and kindness.

As the caretaker of my husband, I had a dark cloud always hanging over me. We knew the grim future, but we never mentioned it. As my thoughts wandered, my way of coping was to take each day as it came, and that seemed to give me the strength I needed

During the first two or three years, there was little obvious change. In fact Pepper's strong, healthy good looks fooled nearly everyone for all five and a half years of his illness. Friends and family, in kindness, tried to tell me the diagnosis was wrong.

My answer was, "But you don't live with him."

It was hard for me to have the patience to bend with his mood changes and his frustrations. He became a man I didn't know. At one point, he said to me. "Betty, please remember. I am not the same man you married." And when things got out of hand I had to constantly remind myself…"He is not himself, he is not himself."

Pepper refused medication of any kind to "cure" his disease. He said there was nothing to help him and he was right.

I went along with him. I never asked for a cure, but I prayed that the disease could be put on hold. He continued to watch sports events enthusiastically. He faithfully attended Princeton football games, and he showed up at Jadwin in the winter to follow women's squash, men's squash, basketball. and wrestling. This was his only hobby, and the winters were long.

The last two years were tough on him. Although he did everything for himself right up until the end…he still drove a car, though slowly…he knew that no matter which way he turned, no matter how very hard he tried, his brain was developing more tangles and more cells were dying. Every single day, as gracefully as he could, he made an enormous effort to look, to act, and to remain the same.

As time passed, it was interesting to see how differently people reacted to a victim of dementia. Some could not face him: they were uneasy and made little effort to converse with him. Others reached out with so much caring, treating him as a normal person. I was so grateful to them. I knew the ones who cared and the ones who moved away. I wondered if Pepper knew, but I never asked.

By this time, he literally could not find things that were right in front of him. His eyeglasses, keys, wallet were relentlessly lost all the time. One day it took him an hour to tie his tie. He had forgotten how and was humiliated. The next day he practiced over and over again.

He couldn't write his name and so he asked me to write out the alphabet in small and capital letters so that he could copy them down and learn again by rote. Reading medical journals and even mysteries finally became too much for him. The brain could not retain "new stuff." Magazines and tidbits of information from the New York *Times* was his limit.

On one occasion, he had an important meeting to attend 15 miles outside of town. As a trustee, he was determined to be there. He was afraid he'd get lost. But he did not want me to drive him. So the day before, he made a dry run and successfully found the meeting place on his own. He came home beaming and drove back the next day.

He avidly watched football, golf and tennis events on TV. In his last year he still played tennis every week, even though his balance was getting bad. He took lessons and learned the two-handed backhand. He tried golf…the driving range was fun for him. But to play on a course was total confusion.

Until he died Pepper still had a brain that worked. He made sense, and he was aware of others' feelings. But increasing bouts of confusion interrupted his train of thought and made him angry. stressful, and sometimes teary. It was a wild circle.

Once, in a moment of frustration, I became the target and he dressed me up and down with some foul words. I told him I was not going to stand for his behavior and *no one* was ever going to talk to me like that. Stunned, he asked, "What did I say? What did I say?"

Last July we moved to Nantucket for the summer, and in August to a house on the water. I knew then that he realized he couldn't do anything right anymore. Things were closing in on him. In spite of his strong self-discipline, he was losing control, losing the terrible battle to stay normal.

As I look back I realize that his last week was different. He was distant and became even more independent of me than usual. He missed an exciting golf tournament on TV because he couldn't read the TV listing. He stopped buying the New York *Times* because he said he didn't need it. He played tennis, rode a bike, threw a football, and ran.

Perhaps he was fitting everything in before he left. We couldn't talk together because he couldn't get his words out. The children were arriving in a few days. and he kept asking when they were coming. He mowed the lawn but zigzagged all over. I told him he should try to mow a straight line and he said, "I am, damn it!" He looked off into space a lot. There was something on his mind. He had a plan. But I wasn't part of it.

One night Pepper went to bed earlier than I. He always went to sleep immediately. But when I arrived upstairs I found him sitting up on the edge of his bed. When I asked him what was the matter, he said, "I can't sleep." Those were his last words to me. The next morning he was gone. His pajamas lay by the door that led to the ocean. That was his message. He had sacrificed himself for all of us, knowing only too well the suffering we would have had to bear had he lived on.

I wish I could have shared his last day and night with him. But if I had, he wouldn't have gone out into the water and I would have ruined his dearest wish and his last brave deed. The children and I have totally accepted the way he died. We all love him and are proud of his great accomplishment, to end his life with dignity as he wanted to.

A friend wrote to me the day after he disappeared; "I want to stand and salute his life and the way he chose to die. I have not seen altruistic confrontation with death of this heroic stature since I was in the Pacific in World War II."

A classmate said, "I'm proud of what my old friend did."

Pepper's brain was sent to Harvard Medical School, where researchers are doing extensive work on Alzheimer's Disease. His brain tissue was so badly affected that pathologists there were amazed that he had had the wherewithal to plan and execute his sacrifice. Yet Pepper won that battle and even in death he made a contribution to medicine. He would have liked that.

The Constables were married for 36 years. She was the longtime women's squash coach at Princeton and her teams and players won championships over and over. Her twin sister and her mother were also squash champions and the Howe Cup in women's competition honors this New Haven family.

Getting Behind The By-Lines

Harvard-Yale Football Program, 1934
Some Sketches of the Gentlemen in the Press Box Whose Writings You Will Read Tonight and Tomorrow
By John D. Moore Jr. and Paul Barnett

If you follow this matter of football in the papers at all, you may want to know something about the men who retail the information about Alma Mater's teams. In the following paragraphs we present a few of the New York, Boston and Connecticut newspapermen who are to be found most consistently in the press stand at New Haven on certain Autumn afternoons.

Robert Fulton Kelley, *New York Times*...One of the lead-off men in the Times batting order. A student of football, rowing and polo. Has published leading books on polo and crew. His "American Rowing" is called the finest on the subject. Works speedily and thoroughly in the course of a game, and writes a well mapped-out news story. Looks more like a young English professor than a sports expert. Secretary of the United States Polo Association. Married and lives in Plandome, Long Island, handy to the major polo fields.

Rufus Stanley Woodward, *New York Herald Tribune*...Considered the most alert of football watchers. Learned the game when he played at Amherst for four years, winning places on the baseball and track teams as well. Started newspaper work as a correspondent at Amherst, went to sea, worked for the Worcester *Telegram* in his home town, went to the Boston *Herald,* and thence to New York. Has published a book on how to watch a football game. Married and lives in New York City.

George Schieffelin Trevor, *New York Sun*...His stories are unrivaled for literary quality and vividness of description. George Trevor knows Yale sports, knows track and field, and golf. Writes them for The Sun, and has a vast following of steady readers, who constantly marvel at his gift for a phrase, his all-embracing vocabulary. Graduated from Yale in 1915. A much-desired magazine writer. Abhors the typewriter of the journeyman reporter. Works with a stub pencil and a pad of foolscap. Literate historian of all college athletics.

George C. Carens, *Boston Evening Transcript*...New England's beloved sage of football, tennis and the general field of amateur sports. Sports editor of the Transcript, he furnishes the Back Bay with keen football diagnosis and a fine sporting page. He can publish the Transcript's Saturday Football Extra while covering a game at Princeton or New Haven. The Harvard squad studies George's analyses of Warren Colby's action photographs of the game, as a regular part of Monday's football practice. Likes to referee professional and Harvard jayvee games. Lives in Arlington, where he is bringing up a large and fine family.

Bill Cunningham, *Boston Post...*Clever, burly critic of college sports and American youth. Widely read throughout New England where his column is as much a part of breakfast as bacon and eggs. Played football at Dartmouth, operated a movie theater to make expenses, and won a Phi Beta Kappa key.

Robert Harron, *New York Evening Post...*Came from the academic walls of Hamline University, St. Paul, Minnesota, where his father taught, to the *Boston Transcript, to* the *Post.* A studious sports writer, who goes into a scholar's research in his work. Writes football, track and polo for the *Post.* A book lover, he wrote a wide-selling work himself on the late Knute Rockne. Married and lives in New York. Thinks hard and loftily and smokes far too many pipes per day.

Paul William Gallico, *New York Daily News...*Brisk commentator on the sporting world, its setting and its people. As well known to the lorgnetted readers of the shiny magazines as he is to the followers of the democratic weeklies and the subway circulation of the *News.* A New Yorker, he went to Columbia and rowed on the crew. Six three and well over two hundred pounds. Keenest interests are his column in the *News,* deep-sea fishing, and the welfare of the Manhattan youngsters whom he develops each year in his Golden Gloves boxing carnival. Lives in New York and Greenwich.

John Kieran, *New York Times...*Has perhaps the most enthusiastic and intelligent following in New York. Writes his *Sports of the Times* regularly and fills it with wisdom, keen observation, satire and such signs of universal erudition as would have qualified him as an editorial writer "on the old

Sun with Dana." Has three brothers working for the *Times.* Their father was President of Hunter College, and reputedly even more learned than his fine son John. John graduated from Fordham and has been reading ever since.

Joseph P. Williams, *New York World-Telegram...*Brilliant sports editor of the flagship newspaper of the Scripps Howard chain. Writes a piercing, philosophical, and withal a good-natured column, different in flavor from anything else in town. An artist at original ideas and newspaper makeup. A booster for the welfare of his beloved Gus H. Fan and all manner of enterprises to help the fellow with two strikes on him. Comes from the Blue Grass country and was an immortal end on the great football machine of Christian Brothers College, Tennessee, in 1917.

Richards Vidmer, *New York Herald Tribune...*"Young Man of Manhattan." Grew up on the Texas border where his father was a general in the Army. Played professional baseball at sixteen, flew a fighting plane, came back and went to college at Georgetown, coached football at George Washington University, worked for the *Times* and now is a leader with the *Herald Tribune.* Good at stories on baseball, boxing, football and golf. Writes short stories and is considering a novel. Lives in Forest Hills.

George Currie, *Brooklyn Daily Eagle...*As far as is known, the only top-notch sports writer who manages to combine his job with that of literary editor and book critic. An unflagging, tireless worker and an unceasing reader. Went to Harvard to study the drama in George Pierce Baker's 47 Workshop. A Yale man can always promote a bet with George

Currie, faithful backer of all his Alma Mater's teams. Lives and reads on Staten Island.

William 0. McGeehan, *New York Herald Tribune...* Laureate of San Francisco's "South of the Slot," official chronicler of the Golden Era of American sport, the Corbett, Fitzsimmons, Matthewson, McGovem days. One of the pioneers in the unmasking business, although several of the younger writers have outstripped him today. Reached a peak when he disposed of an epidemic of fake "ghost-writing" a decade ago by printing a column by Papyrus on the eve of the great match race with Zev. Mrs. McGeehan is a playwright of note.

Westbrook Pegler, *Chicago Tribune Syndicate...* Easterners reading him in the New York *Evening Post* alternately cheer and curse him. *Speaking Out On Sports* is the title of his column, in which you will find him speaking out not only on sports but on the political, economic and the social phenomena in America which catch his penetrating eye. He has uttered in his column some of the finest satire to be found in the papers today. He is dangerous no matter where turned loose, for his eye is unerring in its flight toward the overstuffed and the phony, and he has no qualms at all about telling what he thinks. He has a roving commission to write and may be found anywhere. His father is a newspaper veteran in New York.

Henry Grantland Rice, *North American Newspaper Alliance...*Still writes the most stirring leads of anyone in the press box. His work is found by New Yorkers in *The Sun.* For twenty years a favorite with American sport followers. Writes well on golf and is editor of the *American Golfer.* Contributes to *Collier's* and is well-known on screen and radio. Manages to find time to break 80 in golf. A native Tennesseean, he graduated from Vanderbilt in 1901, having played football and baseball. Has a home and an office in New York, a summer home in Southampton, travels to all the major sporting events, and seems to be at all of those places at the same time. His daughter Florence is well known on the stage.

Harry Cross, *New York Herald Tribune...*Went to Harvard because he thought one wasted one's time at Yale, where his brother spent his spare hours playing the drum in the band. Comes from Connecticut, but not related to the Governor. Got started in his newspaper career when Professor Charles Townsend Copeland (*Copey*) told him to try writing as a profession. Worked in Boston for a while, went to the old New York *Tribune,* became sports editor of the *Evening Post,* then joined the *Herald Tribune,* as lead-off man in rowing, baseball, boxing and amateur sports. Writes the most difficult stories with no outward effort. Lives in the writing colony at Great Neck.

Edward J. Neil, *Associated Press...*Native of Lawrence, Mass. Went to Andover and to Bowdoin, graduating in 1925. He played football at both institutions. On graduation went to work for the AP in Boston and has been there ever since, taking in the major football, baseball and boxing events. Last year he brought honor to the sports writing craft when he won honorable mention for the 1932 Pulitzer prize in journalism. The story was that of a ride down the Olympic Bob Sled Run at Lake Placid as a stowaway on the United States team. The next team down, the Germans, cracked up badly and Eddie was there to help pick them up. Now in the New York office and subject to call to go anywhere.

Alan Gould, *Associated Press*...Combines reportorial, editorial and executive ability in handling his job as sports editor of the largest news association in the world. Gets around the country to all the big sports events, and keeps the organization moving smoothly. Made up his mind to be a newspaperman as an undergraduate at Ithaca, when Peter Vischer told him he'd better give up trying to make the Cornell *Sun* for he'd never make a newspaperman.

George Herbert Daley, *New York Herald Tribune*...Once sports editor of the old Tribune, George Daley is back at the helm of the sports department there. Union College, '92, he was trained to be an engineer, and was scheduled to sail for the tropics on graduation. Instead he reversed his field, got married, and went to work as a newspaperman. Worked for the *Tribune,* the *Morning World,* and now the *Herald Tribune.* More loyal to pure sport than any man in the business. Pond of tennis, football, college sports, and racing. His Sports Talks have a faithful following. Known as the Walter Camp of Union College, for he has fostered the athletics there for over forty years. His home is on Staten Island.

Bert Keane, *Hartford Courant*...Proud of the unique title he once held in the athletic world...Kingpin of American Roller Hockey...Bert Keane's athletic interests are many and strong. Played football, baseball, basketball at Norwich Academy and Springfield College. Among his athletic positions have been Secretary-Treasurer of the Western New England Officials' Association; President Central Connecticut

Football Coaches and Official Association; Chairman of National Challenge Cup Committee of U.S. Soccer Football Association. Worked as sports and later city editor of the New Bedford *Times;* assistant news editor of the Los Angeles *Herald;* sports editor of the Springfield *Republican* and the Waterbury *American.* Strong for golf and has Connecticut's most awe-inspiring slice.

Daniel F. Mulvey, *New Haven Register*...You have been *Looking 'em Over* with Mulvey since 1924, when he decided to forsake the legal department of the New Haven road in favor of the reading public. Dan's job with the railroad was to settle claims. He struck up an acquaintance with some compositors while taking in a burlesque show in the autumn of '24 and was convinced that he ought to become a newspaperman. There was an opening and he applied. He got the job. He is widely read and dotes on covering football, baseball and boxing, but handles well any sporting event to which he, as sports editor of the *Register,* may assign himself.

Robert F. Wilson, *New Haven Journal-Courier*...For years Bob has been in newspaper work in New Haven. From the managing editor's desk of The *Times-Leader,* now gone, he went over to the *Journal-Courier* and embraced his old love, sports. Bob was sports editor of *The Union* also gone, and boasts as fine a background in the field of play as any man in the state. His column *The Morning After* needs only to be read once, to bring that point home. A keen follower of sports, a sharp critic and a good writer, Bob turns out daily, excepting Sunday, two pages well worth while. As secretary of the New Haven Civil Service Commission, he has dovetailed public service and newspaper service to the queen's taste.

Charles E. Parker, *New York World-Telegram*...A reformed city reporter. Graduated in 1913 after playing three years in the Dartmouth line. Tried medical school, and then started a newspaper career with the Boston *American.* Went to the Boston *Post,* New York *Evening Mail,* New York *World* and then to the *World-Telegram* when the *World* was sold. Well known as a tennis writer, but last year Joe Williams switched him to major league baseball, where he starred. Saw great war service with the 5th Division in the Meuse-Argonne.

Allison Danzig, *New York Times*...Quarterbacked with Cornell in '21 and '22. Broke in with the Brooklyn *Eagle,* and then to the *Times.* Experts on tennis in the Summer, football in the Autumn, and the racquet games in the winter. Author of a recent book on court games and considered as the leading authority on racquets, squash, court tennis and their allied sports.

Melville E. Webb, Jr., *Boston Globe*...For forty years Mel Webb has been uttering gospel for Boston readers, and has been quoted by all on the burning matters of big league baseball and Harvard football. One of the real veterans of the business. Writes for the *Sun* in New York now and then and has been syndicated a good deal. Mel is one of the more prosperous of the newspaper fraternity, being able to support town and country homes at one and the same time.

Joe Vila, *New York Sun*...Dean of the New York sports-writers. Bosses the sports department of the *Sun* and writes a daily column. Graduated from Harvard in 1887, and stayed another year in Cambridge to study law. The newspaper business drew him away and he has been in it ever since. Played football and baseball in his Harvard days. Reported football when the reporters walked up and down the sidelines to cover the games and has been present at nearly all the big games, prize fights, World Series and sports meetings in various other lines for forty-five years.

Edwin B. Dooley, *New York Sun*...One of Mr. Vila's bright young men. Chosen as quarterback on several *all Americas* in 1924, when he was writing poetry, calling plays and throwing passes at Dartmouth. Graduated in 1927, and went right to work on *The Sun,* attending Fordham Law School at night. Writes football and track, does some coaching at the Metropolitan colleges and is a popular broadcaster of sporting data.

William J. Slocum, *New York American*...Comes from the nearby village of Winsted, Conn. Started newspaper work in Waterbury and has been with the *Times,* the *Sun* and the *Herald Tribune* in New York. A devoted baseball writer and past president to the Baseball Writers Association.

Burt Whitman, *Boston Herald*...Product of both Harvard and Dartmouth. An ardent follower of baseball and football. Worked on the Worcester *Telegram,* and then the Boston *Traveler* before taking up the job of sports editor of the *Herald.* One of the foremost of the country's baseball scribes and also a past president of their national organization.

(John D. Moore Jr., Yale class of 1934, was an aspiring journalist and Paul Barnett the university's director of sports information.)

Author Bio

William N. Wallace was a sportswriter for New York newspapers for 50 years, the last 35 for The Times before retirement. He is the author of eight books and his prizes include lifetime awards from the Pro Football Writers of America and the College Sports Information Directors. His base is Westport, Conn.

Index

D

E

F

G

H

I

J

K

L

M

N

O

P

R

S

T

U

V

W

Y

978-0-595-35925-7
0-595-35925-6

Printed in the United States
61401LVS00005B/169-240

9 780595 359257